WHO'S GOT THE MONEY?

A Citizen's View of the Grand Fraud

Wall Street is like one giant casino. All the computers are betting tables and poker is the game although craps is more like it. Roll the dice and hope today is your lucky day. Just like we say: "It's in the cards." Somebody wins, somebody loses.

In 2001 we felt like losers. Terrorists destroyed lives and buildings. In 2003 we went to war to beat the terrorists. Maybe to cover up for the costs of war we were given money to spend by our government. We felt on top of the world. A better car, a better house, better clothes, better everything. We were living our dreams. We wanted everything but especially a place called home. Besieged by mail, tantalized by television, everybody was talking about owning a house of their own.

"Could I afford one?" Sure, get one while you can. They're going fast. If you don't like this one, stay for a while and jump to another, probably more expensive, but hey! You're worth it! You've got a job. No problem. We'll make the payments affordable. Heck, in five years the place will probably be worth more than you paid for it. Just sign on this line. Your credit's good. I don't even have to check. Just as long as you're working.

From 2004 to 2007 housing was on fire, so to speak. Three and four offers were being made in a day in some areas of the country. Real Estate was so busy that the only way they knew who was the buyer were the papers with the buyer's signature in the proper places. The banks and brokers were running low on cash because of the volume of sales. The government was standing behind the loans so how could investors lose? Not just any investors but rather the investment funds, the pension funds, the investment banks with large amounts of ready cash where billions could be transferred in an eyelash by a computer. Instead of an individual mortgage being sold, multiple mortgages were bundled together and offered as a package.

Now the bad part starts. Clever greedy businessmen realized that to sell all the mortgages, good and bad, they had to be packaged together in such a way that clever greedy investors would buy them as bundled in hopes that the good ones would overcome the bad ones. And the same ones selling them would buy some themselves.

Sad to say, the investors who could do the best math and were clever in choosing the bundles won and the ones who were blinded by the early results of paper profits lost.

Surprise! Nobody feels sorry for the homebuyers, the ones who bought the supposedly cheap bargains. Talk to them and you find out how sweet the deals were as "Tell us what you can afford and we'll adjust the payments to fit." So the buyers got a teaser rate for the first couple of months, and maybe a year, before the rate got adjusted upwards until they couldn't afford the payments.

If and when the buyers complained about the rate changes, there was no one to complain to because the paper trails of who really owned the mortgage or who was responsible for handling it were completely camouflaged by hundreds of companies having a piece in each mortgage. But the buyer was always known because he was the one whose signature was on almost every sheet of the contract.

The value of the questionable properties is rumored to be two or three trillion dollars but the marketing of the bundles of mortgages runs two hundred trillion dollars. Though some say forty percent of the mortgages are backed by agencies of the Federal government, the attention given to solving the mortgage crisis indicates almost all the mortgages appear to have that backing.

Why weren't the buyers able to make the payments? Since the 1980's wages in the United States have fallen instead of rising for the average worker. Executive pay has skyrocketed 1,000% above the worker's. There is no sorrow for the decline in payrolls. After all, there is need for companies to pay dividends to shareholders in order for them to be attractive to investors. What is hard to understand is where the companies are getting the money if the world's economies are depressed?

True, government has encouraged companies to buy machines to improve productivity and profits. The workers using the machines seem to be paid well, according to their economies, but their use of money isn't improving the economy. Maybe what happened is as the machines improved things, the companies cut back on the number of employees and more and more people had less money because the reason for most foreclosures on houses is no job.

What frightens most economists is the possibility of low employment for many years to come. A memory of the Great Depression of the 1930's is the movies showing people out of work. What put people back to work was preparing for war. Some people still want that solution when they advocate government spending money for international defense. The Space Race owes much to that same reason. More was spent on war than after the war (World War 2) on housing, education, transportation, and better living (food, clothing, cars, appliances, communication). But the World War 2 debt was paid back within a decade after the war because people were working and paying taxes (the Korean War was fought with the surplus from World War 2 for the most part).

Even though most manufacturing is done out of the country nowadays, we have a large service economy in this country. Food, retail, banking, grocery, call centers are examples of a service economy with clerks and operators and clerical the types of personnel. Our service economy has produced many part-time jobs and not so many full-time ones. It has also brought on many independent contractors and consultants that aren't attached to companies and sometimes comprise an army of small individual companies on their own. The results of a service economy is job-hopping (especially for young adults), low wages, and not steady employment. Even large corporations have had lay-offs so there is fear in workers that no career is guaranteed, no job is safe from a termination notice. Because of these fears consumers are trying not to spend any money and are slow to save. So it's not government, not the President, that creates jobs and boosts the economy. Cutback on personnel and panic or near-panic is created.

Between 2000 and 2003 people felt confident. Government gave them back some money, taxes were being cut, most people were working. Terror struck in September of 2001 with hijacked planes flying into buildings or crashing to earth with full loads of passengers. The President rallied the country to fight a couple of wars in the Middle East. One country was quickly overcome, another did not lend itself to immediate victory because of the terrain. Because our military occupied the countries, the cost of maintaining our presence and propping up their economies drained more money from our economy than was expected, if even planned for. No one paid heed to the money being spent because a previous war in Southeast Asia in the 1960's and 1970's seemed to demonstrate that war and prosperity can go together. Defense of our country loosens purse strings. A strong military means many people are employed, either in uniform or in making the goods of war.

The smell of money was thick in our land. The geniuses of Wall Street first experimented with debt instruments of companies. One company borrowing money to buy another company was too simple. Why not take a chance with that debt? Trouble is, companies have accountants who watch over debt very carefully so risks are few and far between. Attention, then, was directed to residential homes as a result of banks realizing that if they accelerated home purchases by loosening up the money supply and granting loans with little or no collateral behind them, the odds might favor defaults. After all, most of the loans were backed by the Federal Government: Fannie Mae and Freddie Mac guaranteed payment at the time of the sale of a property. The loans were so fast and furious that at times real owners of the properties were carelessly or negligently listed on the contracts and nobody cared to be careful and cautious. Buyers were given checks, the original owners paid off their loans and money disappeared in hundreds of companies created to cover the path of the money exchanging hands. What makes this a big jigsaw puzzle is that pension funds, retirement funds, investment funds, and banks using customer deposits all parlayed money into not only buying debt but also into betting on the debts, whether the buyers would continue to pay on the debts or give up and stop or walk away from the properties, letting the banks foreclose on them. It was like one giant card game with the winners being unknown, but few and far between. With nobody admitting to creating the mess and government faced with the collapse of the financial system as a result of a multitude of bad debt, the Government of the United States was requested by the Federal Reserve and Treasury to bail out the financial firms who created the mess in the first place. It's still a puzzlement how, in a country of millions of people, only a few panicked the government. There's never been a true admission of how much debt was handled because, at the time of the bets, the actual amounts couldn't be ascertained due to the enormity of the bets conditional on the dating of the final outcomes.

There was also debt that the government created by giving tax cuts to its citizens and spending on fighting two distant wars. We the people of the United States are blamed for all the debt and are told we have to pay it off. We are talking not millions, not billions, but trillions of dollars. Trying to picture a train with 16,000 boxcars filled with a million dollars each defies the imagination. Yet the debt is even worse because there are amounts still owing to trust funds, pensions, and money market funds.

The Federal Reserve says the money it lent to financial institutions has been paid back and it now has a surplus. Are we missing something? If that is so then why isn't the Federal Reserve paying back the government so the debt is reduced? Maybe Congress has to ask for it back because it's responsible for the budget and debt? One administration spent a lot on tax cuts and wars and didn't admit to its actual deficit, borrowing from foreign governments to cover its rapid expenditures. As a former President said: "It created a mess and didn't admit to it." The financial institutions didn't want to admit to anything either.

Nobody admits that it was one giant fraud. Well, actually, that's two frauds. One by the government and the other by the banks. The government isn't functioning because it doesn't want to do anything about the debt. One side argues for taxes, the other for tax cuts. Neither side admits to the debt being too big to be handled either way. Since the government owes itself about eleven trillion dollars, one way would be for Congress to a) forget about that debt until the five trillion to foreign governments is paid back, or b) declare that debt to be treated like the Marshall Plan, that is, to be paid back slowly after the economy is in full swing again. The derivative bettor would be against both ways because they would say that a country shouldn't welsh on its debt but they forget that in a poker game a debtor is allowed a pass to come up with the money (excluding a time limit unless set).

Wall Street and the banks would not consider this fraud a crime. To them it's just a "moral ambiguity". The traders, acting on behalf of the institutions and involved with other financial institutions and investment companies, overextended the bets and trading. After all, when you bet for all the money in the world, it's easy to get carried away and become lax in due diligence. The prize is so attractive and you're using somebody else's money so a little recklessness is seemingly excusable. Besides, there is insurance to cover some of the loss (if there is any) and huge bonuses if there is a win. Homeowners defaulting on loans is not an everyday occurrence. Remember, though, that the loan packages were prepared for selling, not for quality. Again, a sharp eye and a balky investor were bypassed in favor of a greedy quick-sell. Enter, too, the insurance buffer. Insurance doesn't cover values and only covers a portion of a loss.

So if your investment fails, it's not treated as a complete loss but as a proportion of the value. For example, you invest 80% of your assets and are covered for 20%, figuring to keep the cost of the insurance low over a period of time because you can bail out anytime before a complete loss depending on the availability and the trustworthiness of the information involved. In the case of the home loans, it seems there was no advance warning. Economic collapse and unemployment seem to have happened with trading interruptions and currency devaluations within weeks.

The pension funds and investment banks scrambled to recover from the losses by accepting the insurance payouts with no publicity since the investors would be asking too many questions and might want to pull out of the funds. The funds said they were underfunded for future payouts because of the amount of investors who would be ageing at almost the same time. They so far have been successful in using this explanation. At the same time, their greed has encouraged them to continue in other forms of the derivatives in hopes of winning back their losses. Any government attempt to regulate the derivatives market has been foiled by claims that there are too many methods of handling investments to ascertain if a crime is committed or improper investing occurred.

The cleverness of the scheme to defraud is the use of only one insurance company to provide worldwide backup for the defaults. There has been no explanation so far how the insurance rider was attached to the investment instrument so the question comes up: was the insurance company merely underwriting the certificates or was it at the same time investing in the instruments to compound its own losses or gains? We presume the insured losses have been paid out by the insurance company but that company has not recovered sufficiently even after selling its foreign subsidiary and receiving government financial assistance.

So far, the picture looks complex but the whole idea seems simple. To review the situation in a different light: it started with the Federal Government having a surplus of money. The National Debt was almost non-existent (the trust funds for Social Security and Medicare were made part of the Federal Budget in the 1970's and thought was given in the 1990's to paying off the Treasury Bills that were substituted for robbing the funds to run the government and cover the pork projects the politicians dabbled in).

Regardless of the terrorist attacks in New York and Washington, D.C., the government thought it a good idea to give out hundreds of dollars to its citizens to spend on whatever their fancy and not have to account for it. The economy took a while to heat up because there was a distraction by the start of two wars in distant foreign countries. Shortly after the distraction, the economy did heat up and there followed a housing boom. Why housing? Because it was where big money was made fast.

The realtors blame the buyers, the buyers blame the realtors, economists blame the government, government blames the banks. Whoever blames whomever, a gigantic swindle took place. Pity the poor souls who saw the chance to have a place of their own and were caught up in the rush of greed! Somewhere between the realtors and bankers the boom started. Whether it was the bankers who got the word from the government agencies that they would back any and all mortgages regardless of income verification or the realtors who preached to the buyers that the gold rush was on and within a year or two their house would be worth much more than the price they were paying, the frenzy grew from month to month and year to year until the day the inflated bill was due and the money wasn't there to pay it. Thousands of houses grew to millions of houses that couldn't be paid for and the foreclosure notices filled the mailboxes.

Just before the inflated bills came due, unemployment started to spread. With 1,000 percent pay increases on the executive level and generous dividends to shareholders, as well as dabbling in the derivatives market, companies started to run short of cash. Standard procedure for cutting expenses is laying off large numbers of employees and shifting the workloads to a dwindling number of workers. Stress from getting a pink slip and going on the government dole with few prospects of a choice of jobs, let alone any job available, combined with unpaid bills, credit drying up or rates on cards becoming usurious, added to a further weakening of the economy. The retained employees experienced stress on the job from the increased workload and the sight of empty desks. Instead of collapsing, the economy dried up.

Attention was diverted away from the unemployment happenings by an election year approaching. Even during the pre-election debates, the amount of the Federal deficit was thought to be under a trillion dollars. It wasn't until after the inauguration of the new president that the deficit turned out to be ten trillion dollars. This amount was so horrifying that no one could fathom the enormity of it all. The inefficiency and secretiveness of the previous administration had so camouflaged the deficit that the new administration didn't see a pathway to come up with a solution. One political party wanted to do nothing but stop and cut spending. The new administration sought to prevent further harm to the economy by shoring up the greater part of the automotive industry (the previous administration having bailed out Wall Street firms and major banks by cash infusion) and by legislating changes to health care (weakened in both instances by the defeated political party putting restrictions and delays into the written bills in order to pass them).

The hopes of the voters were so dashed by the ineffectiveness of the new administration to direct the economy to an easy recovery and an end to further unemployment that a couple years later they replaced the conciliatory legislators in Congress with reckless ones who only wanted to be obstinate entrenchers and budget cutters regardless of deficits. However, one must keep in mind that state governments, deep in one party's membership, had so redistricted the population that its party was favored in any election and this effect was primarily responsible for this happening.

The new administration, on the Federal level, did try to control the deficits by cutting spending wherever it could in what are called non-discretionary items like the cost of running the government (limiting the number of Federal employees) but the distant wars raged on and continued to be costly both in lives lost as well as dollars spent. It took two years but one of the wars was ended by bringing the troops home although the costs of having independent contractors providing security for the nascent democracy left behind still weighed on the national budget although not as much as before.

As far as attacking the unemployment problem, one solution proposed is education. We know who should be educated. Firstly, it's all of us in what concentration of wealth means. As the greater population is limited in its earnings, savings, and resources, there is little to almost no movement of money and the few who have the wealth are reluctant or afraid to part with it thereby denying an economy. Secondly, the unemployed have to be given the chance to try something. Some technology companies have found that their employees need to experiment with trying new ways of doing things. If they need help, a team approach with open communication doesn't lead to failure but rather provides for better performance. A good example of this is how we got into outer space. This was a new field (it still is, as in the case of the international space station) but as things were tried, developments advanced. Sure, there were some disasters but such things happen in this human dominated world.

Sure, it cost money but that's part of what is economy. Debt multiples if it isn't being paid for.

Another solution is the creation of new industries to fill the needs of consumers. We mentioned government propping up the old industries like the automotive companies with their hundreds of thousands of workers and in turn their supplier companies with thousands more workers. And yes, government tried to encourage new industries like solar power and electric car companies but questionable management unable to react to competition hinders their profitability and continuance. The problem with government involvement is that government furnishes money and doesn't ride herd over it. Government agencies investigate to prosecute or explain away failure rather than encourage success by monitoring the business plan and operation of the business at least on a quarterly basis and referring academics who are practical-minded and feet-on-the-ground-with-dirty-hands-experienced. Consulting companies have made a good business of working with companies in need of help but they are more concerned with established industries rather than experimental. Academia has been successful in developing new products but it is more interested in obtaining royalties or funds for itself instead of assisting ventures. And banks don't fund experiments, leaving it up to government to do it.

So the question is—what new industries are needed? The answer is---none, until they are invented. In the meantime, our present ones need improvement and jobs should come from them. For the purpose of dealing with them, they can be divided into six basic categories: Communications; Transportation; Environment; Recreation; Entertainment; Daily Living.

1. Communications

Buffalo Bill Cody started as a Pony Express rider in the 1800s. Forty miles at a time to get a letter from one coast to the other. A dangerous job that paid well but lasted no more than five years, replaced by the railroad and the telegraph. The telegraph lasted a long time. Western Union is still in business, though not as in the days of Thomas Edison until his hearing lessened and he experimented with electricity for lights, sound, and motion pictures. Alexander Graham Bell's success with the telephone was due to his ability to monopolize it. The phone exchanges and the exclusive equipment kept competition at bay until the 1970s. The thousands of workers that Edison and Bell utilized for many years were grateful for their employment but their financial gains came from their organizing and strength in numbers compared to the dirty, hard-working miners, oilfield workers, and factory hands who suffered through union-busting and heads-knocking for low wages until they unionized.

Wages and employment flourished in the 1950s and 1960s except for periods of recession brought on by wages not rising fast enough to keep up with demand for goods and services. The golden age of education occurred in the late 1960s and early 1970s when an explosion of students overwhelmed the schools and young college graduates found teaching jobs all over America. The economy was so overheated that in the late '70s inflation ran rampant and competition started to affect companies and their products. When the government put the brakes on the economy in the 1980s, companies reacted by cutting employees and ridding themselves of subsidiary companies. Color TVs and private phones subtly changed society by making everyday news more relevant and the computer came along to offer new vistas into handling myriads of information and compressing it by shrinking it as well as performing multiple operations with fewer people. No longer do oceans or land masses deter us from worldwide communication and instantaneous information because we've penetrated outer space. Youth has profited from the Internet but not enough to effect the economy except in scattered pockets of the country. Keep in mind, too, that not everyone needs to be in the same industry or have the same interests.

2. Transportation

Not everyone wants to be a bus or truck driver. There are ships and planes, trains and trolleys, vans and taxis, and everybody still wants their own car, bicycle, or motorcycle. But who's going to invent the best moving sidewalk and who will own the company that runs it? Who can come up with the best way of ridding a road of ice and snow?

Transportation has to do with moving people and goods. The means of moving each has provided thousands, if not millions of jobs to make the vehicles, build and maintain the roads and tracks, the runways, stations and airports, the planes and ships, and the fuels to run them. We've come a long way from the horse and buggy but we've almost given up on space exploration and planetary development. Maybe the spaceships need to be made of elements from another planet but how will we get them or make products there? How will we get the workers and the equipment there? What currency will we use and who will invest in the enterprises? If we need forward thinking for such ventures, why can't we come up with solutions for our present problems? The space race of the twentieth century provided employment for thousands of people and now do we want to let decay inhabit our thinking and existence? Competition with a foreign country provided the impetus in the past. Just a goal gets a nation going.

3. Environment

Right away, everybody thinks about air, water, earth, and fire. From the days of living in a cave, the problem has always been shelter. Trying to sleep in the rain or cold without a tent or some means of cover makes us aware of our fragile existence. If we build a house, we rush to get it covered before we start working on the interior. Then we want to put in wires for electricity and pipes for water and to carry off sewage.

When Edward Land came up with a way to eliminate utility meters, he soon found that if he didn't change his thinking he would be out of a job. His idea was to put solar cells on every roof so a house would generate its own electricity. Instead, he went on to develop the electric eye for opening and closing doors and the Polaroid camera for developing quick pictures. The lesson is that established industries want to protect themselves instead of innovating.

Our modern society has set up desalinization plants in other places of the world while we contend with limited resources for ourselves. We continue to want to live on landfills or pollute the air with burning garbage while we still entertain the idea of sending it to outer space.

Conservation has to do with safeguarding the environment. We will be out of oil and gas by the end of this century. Every day almost a quarter of a million persons are born into this world. We must develop new ways to heat and cool, provide electricity more efficiently, and keep our waters clean and healthy for all species. We need monitors, technicians, and developers as well as trained employees to maintain even our present systems. Having had a limited contact with waste disposal and water quality in my younger days, my experience impressed me with the necessity to take action and make decisions quickly because sewage handling plants and water purification plants are outdated from the day they start and the volume they handle is greater than originally planned. The costs of safeguarding the environment take years to show benefits and future generations enjoy them rather than current ones.

4. Recreation

Even when there's snow and cold, people find ways to enjoy the season. One must wonder though if obesity is a problem, what are people doing for exercise? Outside of professional performers in sports, there seems to be little outside activity of the general population and too much stay-at-homeness or working too many hours and not enjoying life. Recreation seems to be one area where, except for paid professionals, most jobs are part-time, seasonal, and low paying, if not on a volunteer basis. A vibrant economy is necessary for this category to be doing well for the general population.

5. Entertainment

Like Recreation, Entertainment has been harmed by the poor economy. Electronic gadgetry influences our lives and provides news, entertainment, and communication for a large share of our population. Companies in this field have spent much of their time and money in recruiting new customers and trying to retain the ones they have rather than developing new productions to appeal to general audiences. In other words, they're after a "quick buck". Numbers such as for ratings and subscribers or viewers drive profits and plans with quality of works suffering in too many instances. The publishing and broadcasting industries are most notable examples. These industries sell content which means they need writers, marketers, and sellers as well as production technicians and producers who are financial arrangers to cover the cost of producing content or for finding and developing content. There used to be something like a training program in these industries but the desire for immediate profit has eliminated preparation and development. This seems to be a widespread problem with American business today.

Newspapers used to have junior reporters and established columnists. Television had several writers at least to come up with multiple ideas and scripts. Book publishing pushes best-selling authors but fiction is either murder mysteries or romances and nonfiction is politics, wars, and how to succeed in business (it seems to mimic movies and newspapers). Whether television, movies, books, magazines and newspapers, or internet, costs shrink profits and old ways are derided because profits today are measured in billions rather than millions of dollars. The old way was to cover failure and loss by successful content that overproduced and kept repeating interest and sales. The merging of companies in the entertainment field has brought in executives and managers that aren't familiar with the old way or don't accept it. Entertainment needs more people to work in it and the old way is still the way to go because of the fickleness of the general public.

There are numerous examples of overwhelming success in television and movies, less so in print although one popular author has managed to put together a stable of writers who produce and he puts his name with them to generate the sales that afford all of them to live comfortably. Scientific analysis or attempts at it have proven disastrous in trying to predict public moods and desires.

6. Daily Living

This category encompasses housing, health, food and clothing. Whether renting or owning, people need some kind of shelter. Even homeless people will use an overpass or even a cardboard box or just a coat or blanket to provide protection. Even in war, a hole in the ground and some bush or tree cuttings overhead are comforting. So when a giant fraud occurs that takes advantage of peoples' desire for a house, everyone's sense of justice should be aroused and remedies sought to deal with the problem forthwith. But the gigantic scope of this tragedy has been expanded by further greed and lack of consideration. Even buyers from other countries are gobbling up the supply of foreclosed homes in this country with all cash sales, pushing out people trying to buy a familial home because greed sees a future windfall of outrageous profit for an investment combine acting like a scythe to cut down all other deals and consideration.

Housing has shown us the greatest pain of unemployment. Not only are the homeowners who have lost their jobs hurting, but also the people who build homes, buildings, bridges, roads, and structures are out of work. Repeated entreaties to bankers and politicians to put these people back to work fall on deaf ears because the thinking is "if nothing is done about it, the problem will eventually go away". Though their words may not say it, their actions prove it.

History repeats itself. In 1937, just as the President's steps to overcome the Great Depression seemed to be working, his political opponents and the financiers complained mightily in the information mediums about the amount of government expenditures being used to seemingly no avail and caused the drying up of further efforts to work a way out of further calamity which then led to the great migration which lasted until 1970. The Savings and Loan Scandal of the 1980s had a similar migratory effect.

The worst nightmare is a return to the Age of the Moguls, roughly 1880 to 1910, when we had a large influx of immigrants and people were herded into "factory towns". We hear of the Gay 1890s and the erecting of multi-story buildings in expanding cities but we have to delve into history to find the stories of the Robber Barons who coddled government to garner vast fortunes from coal mines, shipping industries, meat packing plants and clothing factories, retail emporiums, without hindrance of laws and concern for families and workers paid in low wages and oftentimes charged back for expenses incurred by furnishing them with food, clothing, and housing while the Barons lived in luxury and left behind estates worth millions. Is it any wonder that the workers fought to improve their lot, finally realizing the only way to get improvements was by uniting together to be numerous enough to demand and secure benefits as a result of their labor?

Housing is like the automobile industry. Housing and Transportation account for the majority of jobs in our present culture. They have supplier and service companies that expand employment to many states and cities and they require banks, insurance companies, and maintenance and repair enterprises, as well as dealers and sales offices to satisfy and garner customers. Government is necessary not only to regulate them but to uphold them because the collection of taxes is required of them as part of running an economy. When taxes are affected by a down economy, then it's necessary for government to act to restore employment and employers but not investors because risk is their governance.

During and after World War Two, large employers saw the need for healthy employees to maintain production and profits. Most contracted with insurance companies who in turn contracted with doctors and hospitals to service those employees and their families. Little must be credited to enlightened owners and management and much to unions for this provision for today many companies are avoiding health care for their employees with the excuse of the expense of it interfering with their profit picture and return to their shareholders while burdening their employees with it and risking poor attendance and individual as well as family health problems and financial bankruptcies.

Government is starting to step in to provide some form of health care to a greater percentage of the nation's population but, due to the ignorance of many politicians who don't realize that keeping everybody healthy eliminates many getting sick and costing everybody more, the delay is adding years to tackling the problem and controlling costs.

In the meantime, the need for people to work in health care is growing daily and training is needed for this workforce. Our germ-laden hospitals need their maintenance staff educated about proper cleaning materials and machines; hospitals' and doctors' offices and clinics' staffs about computers and record-keeping and billing; patient care personnel about assisting and caring for patients; home care and long term care givers in patient handling and caring methods. Doctors and nurses and medical technicians receive extensive training. Now it's time for all in medical care to be trained because better care cuts costs as we're seeing with the implementation of the Affordable Care Act. Hospital Administrators need to be trained in accounting and management, if not already, in order to handle increased patient loads as well as additional service personnel.

The hospitals trying to control costs should be appreciated for their lobbying of state governors and legislators to take advantage of the Federal government's monetary help to expand health services to the financially disadvantaged. The hospitals probably are aware of the August 1999 issue of the Journal of the American Medical Association regarding a 1994 study of the number of gun related deaths and emergency treatment of non-fatal wounds of persons treated. In that study, it was noted that for every person dead from a gunshot, two are wounded and the cost for emergency treatment ran 2.3 billion dollars with the government paying $1.1 billion of that (or 49%). Still, gun violence ran third for emergency cases after poisoning and motor vehicle accidents. Nevertheless, the problem is worsening with 31,076 homicide and suicide deaths in 2010 with 73,505 treated for gunshot wounds. Back in 1994, people with private insurance accounted for only 18% of the cases paid that way. That study further found that the costs of treatment after release from the hospital were greater than the costs of emergency treatment in the hospital.

Healthcare should not be treated as a business because there is no choice. If you're sick and don't take care of yourself, odds are that you will get worse and the cost of treatment will be more. Better lifestyle choices can help in maintaining good health but genetic diseases from several generations back can interfere in our daily living. Because of the volume of patients treated, recovery from gunshot wounds has greatly improved as emergency staffs have learned on the job how to better handle them. We don't need more gun violence but we do need more training and more staffs in healthcare.

The food industry has a large number of low-paying jobs. It used to have steady employment but as employees have unionized, companies have cleverly revised work schedules and cut back on the number of employees ostensibly to maintain profits but senior management positions' pay ranges have greatly increased as in much of American industry today.

Whether in fine dining restaurants or fast food chains, cooks, waiters, and cashiers are generally very poorly paid. Because of people contact there is some satisfaction in spite of long or irregular hours, standing for long periods of time, a mad dash to handle a rush of hungry and demanding customers, and a flurry of serving dishes or containers. But people have to eat so it's a chance for first job, any job, and more action than thinking. Owners get rich but employees and managers don't. In a tight economy a job can be hard to come by because of the volume of seekers of employment. Many of these establishments are truly small businesses like many family farms that have to compete against factory farms and giant food factories that still are reminders of Sinclair Lewis' book "The Jungle". The goliaths of mass food production in this day and age are like mechanized slave factories employing Asian and minority populations hoping by their labors to someday save enough to obtain a bit of the American dream to rise in economic status and enjoy better living. Our economy is dependent on these people to handle our hunger and variety of foodstuffs. The hue and cry for government deregulation in this industry does lead to public awareness when food contamination causes the illness of thousands in multiple states due to mass distribution but no real reform or strict adherence to regulations seems to result. The markets where people shop love to advertise their wares but decline any responsibility for what is delivered to their stores. This industry is definitely tied to healthcare and both are essential elements of the national economy.

Despite toothpick-thin models walking the runways at fashion shows and movies of leading men and women in fashionable ensembles, the general public dresses up for fewer social events in these times and more often for the weather, the job, and for casual living. The economy can slow the purchase of clothing but until nudity is made lawful, there will always be clothing bought for young and old.

Since almost all manufacturing of clothing has been arranged for in foreign countries, there are very few jobs in this country involving the manufacturing of cloth and clothing. Like the design and engineering of automobiles, so the design of clothing affords those with artistic talent to be able to find employment in this industry as well as salespeople, warehouse workers and retail clerks. Contrary to what occurred during the Great Depression of the 1930s, the price competition and low profit margins are causing brick and mortar shopping to be under assault by warehouse operations utilizing the internet and home delivery to satisfy customer needs. With few tailors and seamstresses available, and inexact sizing to accommodate the myriad of body types, the problem of returns besieges these mass marketing operations. Attempts to solve measurement by computer have not succeeded, even with thousands of points of reference on a male or female body. Adding to this is the desire to try items on while shopping in a public milieu and leaving the confines of house or apartment. The economy and jobs are essentials in any social setting. Changes in our ways of living are taking place regardless of conventional attitudes and activities. Not only is employment changing but how to get better employees needs consideration.

To understand employment trends and practices, it's necessary to go back in time to the great migrations from Europe into the United States in the 1890s and through the 1910s. Industrialization began with the invention of the steam engine but mechanization started during the Civil War with the production of weapons for the conflict. Not only was the difference in guns but also in uniforms. The Northerners wore blue wool uniforms made in the factories and mills of New England whereas the Southerners wore homespun everyday work clothes usually made of cotton, thanks to Eli Whitney's cotton gin made to remove the seeds from the cotton balls picked from the fields of plants nurtured by slaves.

With the explosion of population caused by immigration, more goods and resources were needed. The ones who had made money from the war or were fortunate enough to convert an idea into an industry took advantage of this explosion to set up company towns where a workforce could be housed, raise a family, and repay their employer for everything he provided them with, food, clothing, housing, and work and living utensils. A company town was a benevolent enslavement that lasted through World War 1 and beyond, until in the 1920s the postwar economy developed installment buying and the automobile and radio changed the culture of the times.

Because of the Great War, soldiers had money in their pockets and when they returned back to their jobs, they demanded more money and their employers paid it because the economy was heated up due to over 3 million men returning to their country. The automobile freed the workers to go elsewhere to seek work and a different place to have a home, to get an education, and to have a hospital where doctors could care for them and their families. The radio gave the worker and his family news and entertainment, told him of sales and reminded him of the bonus a veteran of military service in the Great War was entitled to, even though it was initiated by Congress in 1924 and never paid until 1936 when that $1,000 alleviated some of the pain of the Great Depression and caused a baby boom.

Even though wages dropped dramatically in 1930 and a great migration occurred within the country because of home foreclosures, the Dust Bowl wiping out many family farms, an over 25% unemployment rate, and bank failures causing many people to lose their life savings, the country survived and the election of 1932 brought a President and Congress that instituted a minimum wage law, a Civilian Conservation Corp that employed not only 25,000 married and under age 40 war veterans but also many hundreds of thousands of unemployed single men under age 25 who were wandering the country in search of jobs and who would be most of the soldiers enlisted in the beginning of World War 2. The government also put into law new regulations for industry to make for safer workplaces and allowing unions so that wages and benefits could be improved. The downturn of the economy in 1937 wasn't due to the government doing too much but rather by government doing too little as a result of the opposing political party complaining about any government assistance to the downtrodden.

World War 2 demanded a change in the workforce. So many men were needed for a two front war that women were attracted to the factories by high wages and overtime hours in order to win the war by overproducing the enemy. When the war ended and the soldiers returned home, the government not only paid them for their years of service but also provided them the opportunity to expand their education at government expense. As a result, employers not only had a huge manpower pool to choose from but a well-educated workforce to work in the factories and businesses and to manage them as well. Prosperity brought on huge housing tracts, three and four children families, more schools, health insurance resulting from the need for a healthy workforce during the war, cars for transportation to work and social activities , labor-saving devices for home and business, leisure time to enjoy neighborhood and town activities and entertainment, and new ways of communication by phone, radio, and television. Prosperity was so bounteous that it allowed for rebuilding our allies and enemies as well.

These idyllic times were sometimes interrupted by downturns in the economy called recessions – not enough goods or not enough money to satisfy demands. Recessions brought on rearrangements in the workforce. At first, recessions caused a temporary pause in hiring employees. A year or two at most and then the economy got back on track and employment recovered. Then, in 1981, the government jumped on the brakes and dried up the money supply by dropping interest rates. The economy froze up, unemployment spread and businesses thought of other countries to cut their labor costs and develop new markets. The joke before was the U.S. had too much of everything and the rest of the world lacked the ingenuity to invent and prosper. From 1984 on, large corporations started to concentrate on improving the overseas factories they used to manufacture goods for worldwide markets and keep labor costs low. Some foreign companies took over some American factories and, if they didn't out the unions, they weakened them by skillful tactics to cut labor costs. The American public generally takes little interest in trade imbalances and currency fluctuations but Wall Street pays close attention to them because the American economy is now part of the worldwide economies. Economists still fight over whether there should be a return to the gold standard but the total of the economies far outstrips whatever value could be put on the metal.

From the 1980s on, large corporations have had to deal with worldwide employment. Even though America is a land of many cultures, business is not acquainted with other cultures. Besides language barriers, there is a lack of understanding of how other people think. What's happened to employment, even locally, is a fear of competency. The initial reaction to this fear, on the part of business, is to involve more people in the hiring process by arranging for a committee with multiple viewpoints to decide on a candidate. Since this method has proven to be more time-consuming and ineffectual in decision-making, now there is concentration on the steps in the hiring process in hopes of providing for the diversity of cultures and the mobility of interviewing devices.

Candidates for employment can either apply in person, mail in a resume or application or videotape, or on the internet by submitting a resume or doing a live presentation with

17

a video camera in which they can relate their background and talents. From the information provided, the company gleans whether the candidate has the experience and motivation from previous employment, the education to learn a job, and the ability to succeed in the position available. After a candidate is chosen for consideration, a hiring source in the company contacts the candidate to either have him or her tested at that time or to set an interview either in person or on the phone or on the internet.

The purpose of testing a candidate is to assess either their general intelligence or their type of personality. A general intelligence test would consist of language ability and simple math. These areas could be expanded to include matters of interpretation, word meanings and story outcomes. The math could involve story problems, shapes, sizes, and measurement. Personality tests cover general social likes and dislikes, sometimes what would you do type situations, or behaviors in reaction to other peoples' actions. The tests should lead to questioning in the interview during which education and experience can be delved into as a prelude to ascertaining personality, reasoning, and motivation in more depth. Because of the diversity of cultures, more latitude should be encouraged in initial evaluation. Success in business is a result of teamwork and, with people of diverse cultures working together, background is more important than I.Q.s. Women managers may react differently than men in certain situations. A technology problem may need more than technical ability for solution. Cold or flu may hinder performance so health is an important consideration. Even work settings play a role in performance. Everyone wants a corner office rather than a work carrel. Most importantly, is guidance provided on the job to develop better performance and assess performance more concretely? All of these help the executive and managerial levels to better match the personnel to company projects like developing new products, better customer service, and opening new markets.

Up until the mid 1980s, a company based its hiring decision on what pay the candidate had been getting from his previous employment or on what it would cost to hire the potential employee. In the late 1980s, company hiring changed to how cheaply a candidate could be hired. What caused this change in thinking goes back to the 1950s when the minimum wage was 75 cents an hour in 1955 and a dollar an hour in 1956. This was a confirmation of a bare existence for an individual. In 54 years, we've only gotten to $7.25 an hour which amounts to $15,080 a year and that is less than unemployment compensation of $300 a week which amounts to $15,600 a year and less than a private's pay in the army, $16,794 in 2009 and $18,192 in 2013 (both excluding room and board).

It's not that the worth of a worker is less. Even with low wages in the 1950s and 1960s there was prosperity (excluding a recession in the cusp of the fifties and sixties). Prosperity continued through the 1970s with interest rates rising to 9%. Then in March 1979, to thwart inflation, the Federal Reserve Chairman cut the money supply causing the interest rates to rise in 8 months from 9% to 15%. In 1980, the new President and Congress rushed in to help, making new laws that changed the Savings and Loan industry drastically.

They began by granting the Savings and Loans the power to invest in real estate loans anywhere by allowing dual charters for the associations. No longer was a S&L Association limited to a particular state. They could cross state lines, branch into other states, make risky investments (they could treat 40% of their assets as commercial real estate whether they were or not), their FDIC insurance premiums were kept low, and any losses would be covered by the Federal taxpayers instead of being regulated by any state. In 1981, Congress eliminated interest rate restrictions which now allowed adjustable rate mortgages to be transacted. In 1982, Congress eliminated the "due on sale" clause which meant the seller could no longer pass onto the buyer the old interest rate on a mortgage.

By the end of 1982, the market value of homes had dropped by 100 billion dollars and the Savings and Loans lost 9 billion dollars in assets. Because now the Federal taxpayers had to take the losses, a secondary mortgage market was created with Fannie May and Freddie Mac, the Federal mortgage guarantors, cutting mortgage rates and beginning to squeeze the S&Ls out of existence. One of the last to go, Washington Mutual, was made into an investment bank when Congress in 1994 allowed banks to do interstate branching.

Following the S&Ls fiasco came the "Junk Bond Kings" of the 1990s. Any company could be attacked and taken over by another if the investment could be sold on a high risk probability of success. So what if the risk of failure of the business was greater than that of success? A higher rate of return promised for the investment would be accomplished by good old-fashioned American ingenuity. A company just needed the right management to turn a poor performer into a gold mine of returns. The thrill of success swept through Wall Street like a tidal wave. What did it matter how much you were investing if the rate of return was 15% or better? Guarantees? What company couldn't do better with newer equipment, better thinking, newer markets? Expansion was the name of the game. Diversity was necessary to penetrate new markets. Adding more companies would spread the risk. Such were the paeans of the bond sellers.

Where junk bonds gave false returns, there began in 1987 instruments of financing

that furnished promised returns. Drexel Burnham Lambert marketed something called a

credit default operative which by 1997 expanded into a derivatives market. The value of

a derivative is derived from the value of other assets. These other assets are arranged into

tranches (categories) with quants (units) which create and distribute cash flows. By

developing complex algorithms to protect against risk, some quants can have losses while

other quants can have gains thereby insuring against total loss. The theory is that a

probable default can be gambled upon with a fair amount of success if investors take into

account the percentage of defaults over a given period of time with an accounting of the

quants success rate based on the assumptions of the factors involving the quants and

depending on whether the CDOs are from an index or actual securities or are cash

instruments. The total price rests on the number of possible defaults in each tranch and

the accumulated value assumptions. The buyers of these CDOs were limited to only

hedge funds, commercial and investment banks, and pension funds. The total market is

estimated to be over 200 trillion dollars.

Like poker or a roulette wheel, the financial risks of success or failure are dependent

on assumptions and a certain time of happening. These bets cost billions of dollars and

many investors have lost so much money that financial ruin is threatening large firms if

not countries. Worldwide currency markets, if not bet upon, are thrown into turmoil

because of the large sums being used in this market. To give two examples, let's observe

the economies of Japan and the U.S.A.

With their meticulous planning, the Japanese automotive and equipment companies

penetrated foreign markets even greater than their expectant dreams. Knowing their past reputation for products was deemed cheap and faulty, Japanese engineers and industrialists concentrated on improving designs and quality of products that would change not only impressions but would capture entire markets. Even using remelt steel, their automotive, construction, and industrial machinery products along with their consumer electronic products helped them become the third largest economy in the world. Workers' wages kept going up so spending rose while at the same time, being an intelligent people, the saving rates encouraged people to put money aside for the future. The economy overheated and the government, fearing things were getting out of control, cut the interest rates, fought the unions to lower wages, cut or eliminated pensions, and prevented savings from easily moving from one institution to another. All this was done to weaken the yen which was well over 100 to the dollar. This helped their export market and discouraged their import market. Within their own economy, the yen was worth less and spending decreased. Deflation reigned for over a decade. Because of natural disasters, the yen has strengthened due to currency speculators thinking the Bank of Japan would have to print more money to cover the losses and so the speculators started buying yen, thereby forcing the bank to increase the money supply. The yen is again hovering around 100 to the dollar but the Bank of Japan is closely monitoring the interest rates to try and keep the yen strong enough to maintain the export markets but weak enough to control the imports and stabilize land and housing values. The excuse of an ageing population on the economy is rarely heard now since the natural disasters and the import-export markets have taken over the news and the interest of the banks.

The reason for considering the Japanese and U.S. economies is not only their size but because they are the only two of the G-8 economies that are not bound by treaties or obligations that would prevent them from turning on their printing presses and printing enough money to cover their debts. In Japan, the Bank of Japan controls the interest rates; in the U.S., the Federal Reserve not only controls interest rates but has been buying Treasury bonds to filter money to the banks to try and stimulate the economy. In all economies, the value of currency depends on the value of the workers (their wages, benefits, pensions). Workers' value is increased by unionization, not by individual bargaining, as evidenced by the fact that womens' wages are below that of male workers and, as we've seen especially since the 1970s, hourly pay is far behind executive remuneration. In the U.S. and Japan economies, the banks and government have cut interest rates, the wages of workers have been lowered, workers' pensions and savings plans have been cut, modified, or eliminated, and the dollar and yen are being manipulated in the currency markets by speculators. Government, in both economies, can't enforce criminality because the regulators didn't act on the undue risks before they collapsed or took place so the evil-doers continue without fear of prosecution. Even the rating agencies, Moody's, Standard&Poors, and Fitch, have been suspected of collusion with some Wall Street firms but the evidence is insufficient for bringing them into court. Many large corporations, being customers of banks participating in the derivatives market and believing the ratings ascribed by the agencies to the values of the credit default swaps, joined the banks in purchasing these instruments and we have heard of a few successes but nothing of the failures. The question still persists: will the government have to rescue a multitude of losers as it did in 2008? When corporations rid themselves of 10 or 20% of their employees in order to maintain an attractive bottom line, there has to be fear of incompetence developing. Competence comes on employees staying in the company and on the job as long as possible. Right now only 50% of employees are deemed competent but all can be trained to develop competency if a company expends the funds and will to do so. The area of greatest complaint is customer service.

Instead of being accused of being criminals, Wall Street would prefer to blame taxpayers for creating the SWAPS market. From the earliest days of the stock market there have been stock frauds: schemes to make sometimes fictitious companies appear to be money-makers with solid stock offerings. In the 1920s, the stock market flourished amid the prosperity resulting from the end of World War 1 so that even the common person was buying shares of stock in any company. It has long been held that the reason for the Wall Street crash in October, 1929 was due to the brokers calling in the loans that were extended to buyers of stock (also known as margin calls). The buyers didn't have the cash to pay the loans and the stocks lost value. As companies' securities fell, bank portfolios wasted away, depositors panicked and made runs on the banks. Over 9,000 banks failed. To prevent an outflow of gold (the U.S. was one of a few import-export countries still on the gold standard), the Federal Reserve raised interest rates while the government passed the Smoot-Hawley Tariff to cut imports because wages rose in 1930 and 1931 and production was falling as well as prices. Trying to maintain profits and pay dividends, companies laid off workers because customers weren't buying products and prices were being cut. The U.S. suffered a major drought and many farmers lost their farms and migrated out of the Mississippi Delta (the tragedy is known as the Dust Bowl). With 25% unemployment, the U.S. had a Great Depression.

In the 1920s, though Wall Street encouraged reckless speculation, the government took a *laissez-faire* attitude towards business and caused deficits that hindered any recovery. We've seen Wall Street's progression from stock speculation to real estate bubbles and company takeovers involving junk bonds and now the derivatives market. A close look at the 1920-1921 depression provides a study of government boondoggles.

From 1896 to 1919, inflation was a problem in the U.S. The price rises from 1914 to 1920 forced the iron and steel workers, the coal miners, and the railroad workers to demand higher wages and when they weren't coming, their unions went on strike at the end of 1919 and the beginning of 1920. The Federal Reserve, established in 1913, raised the interest rates in 1919 from 4% to 7% to slow inflation. The unions won the wage increases but when the companies went to the banks for loans, they were denied. Investment dropped, people stopped buying, depositors ran on the banks, banks failed, and unemployment rose.

In 1921, President Harding got Congress to vote for the Fordney-McCumber Tariff which cut imports but allowed foreign exporting countries (which were going off the gold standard to allow their inflationary economies) to pay the U.S. in gold (which ballooned the U.S. gold holdings to 40% of the world's supply). Harding cut taxes (but added more lower incomes to the tax rolls) and cut interest rates, which stopped the Depression. Harding's successor, Calvin Coolidge, kept the brakes on the economy and maintained low taxes and low spending.

In 1921, Harding's Commerce Secretary, Herbert Hoover, organized the top businessmen in the country to deal with the unemployment problem that the Depression created. The Conference arranged for the government to grant relief only to the states and cities where unemployment was the greatest and the economies there were able to weather the downturn and turn around faster when the Depression ended.

When Hoover followed Coolidge, the economy overheated and we saw how the stock market crash, the bank failures, the cut in consumer spending, the Dust Bowl, and the Smoot-Hawley Tariff brought on the Great Depression. When Hoover cut the tax rates, the government deficits rose, the reason being that this was done to prevent the outflow of gold (to pay for imports rather than to provide financing for investment). As the economist, Michael Bernstein, argues – the investment problems retarded the recovery because older industries couldn't generate sufficient investment while newer growing industries had trouble obtaining investment funds in the depressed environment. By the time Hoover raised the rates, consumers had stopped spending and the depression got even worse.

When President Franklin D. Roosevelt, who followed Hoover, took over in 1932, his advisors advocated the changes he made that started the country on the road to recovery. But they failed him in his second term by cautioning that more shouldn't be done. Preparation for war loosened spending and probably helped Congress to pass a $240 billion war budget in 1942. The steel, aviation, and shipbuilding industries vastly expanded because of that. Because the military took most of the young men for service, the 50 and 60 year old men were left to work in coal mining, running the railroads, and making steel. Is it any wonder that there were 20,000 labor disputes and a 3 to 17% truancy rate in those industries during the war? Wages only increased one-tenth of what they were in 1930 while the work week was lengthened to 48 hours (and 60 hours in capital industries). Even many young women came into military service so there was a labor shortage beginning in 1943. Price levels were not allowed to rise but consumer goods were almost non-existent even for a couple of years after the war ended.

After having the only president ever elected to four straight terms, the voters considered his successor, Harry Truman, capable enough to finish the war, restore the enemies, Japan and Germany, and our European Allies through the Marshall Plan, and fight a war in Korea while bringing down the national debt. Surprisingly, Truman got Congress to allocate funds for improvements in national defense before he was defeated in an election that Dwight Eisenhower, a hero of World War 2, promised the people he would end the war in Korea and then sold the taxpayers on the need for a national road network to help in the event the U.S. was ever invaded by an enemy. Both Truman's and Eisenhower's final budgets were for defense projects that were carried out after their terms were over.

President John F. Kennedy energized the nation with the idea of exploring space and President Lyndon Johnson is known as a leader who thought he could have a butter and bullets economy while fighting the Vietnam War. The nation voted in President Richard Nixon to see an end to that war. Besides being the only president to resign from office, he is considered the door-opener for China to take its place in the world. But he left office four years before China opened itself to foreign investment. A little insight is needed here to realize how China has become the second biggest economy in the world. Most of the history related here is from the Foreign Policy Institute and the statistics are sourced from the CIA World Fact Book.

When the Chinese "volunteers" overran the American lines in Korea in December, 1952, the U.S. military found the Chinese troops were using Russian made weaponry and fighting on a cup of rice a day. After a Korean truce was declared, the "volunteers" returned to their homeland and took up what most of the country was doing- trying to raise enough food to stave off starvation.

Mao Tse Tung was finally in control of the entire country of China by 1958, at which time he began his "Great Leap Forward" program to communize the people. Landlords turned over their lands to the "communes" – no longer was there supposed to be private ownership. The party structure did have bosses to make sure assigned quotas were met. But Mao couldn't eliminate corruption, which was a characteristic engrained into Chinese society, so that when the plans weren't working out, excuses were bountiful but food was scarce. In 1960, famine dominated the land and huge numbers of the population died. The central government promised reforms and in 1966 a "Cultural Revolution" took place, dominated by the Red Guards, zealous youths who used Mao's "Little Red Book" as a bible to preach Mao's ways to change society.

How enough people survived the twenty years of disaster until 1980 is a miracle that that generation doesn't want to talk about or remember. But in 1978, when foreign investment started in, capitalism looked very promising as a philosophy that might fit into Chinese society inasmuch as industriousness helped people survive in all of China's history.

Mao Tse Tung was gone. Now Deng Xiaoping talked of reforms to the economy. Private enterprise was allowed with small to medium size businesses developing. Even the dissidents in Taiwan trusted the change and started many of their factories on the mainland. Regardless of the Communist takeover under Mao, Hong Kong and Macau continue to operate independently of the rest of China and they do business on their own with the World Trade Organization, the Asian-Pacific Economic Council and the World Credit Organization.

Since almost 30% of the population lives below the poverty level, the government made welfare a cost of production and it is taken out before taxes are paid to the state. But three large enterprises were kept as state-owned businesses, namely, the power grids and two petroleum operations. These enterprises are run by families of the ruling party leaders who amassed vast fortunes from the corruption that is practiced as a result of the state making five year plans and production falling short of the plans because of overly ambitious goals and payoffs to cover up the losses. Fifty percent of the state-owned businesses that were failing because of bad loans and payoffs were privatized in 2000 to make them profitable. The remaining businesses still under state plans are allowed to have their managers devise the means to achieve their production and have to answer for it. The state still gets 43% of its capital from these monopolies. The state also invested in long term foreign securities to weather downturns in the economy.

The advent of capitalism in China didn't solve the food problem. There was rationing of commodities until 1986. And though there was a 10% growth rate in the economy from 1980 to 2010, the Peoples Congress in 2004 made four important resolutions:

1) reduce unemployment which in 2003 ran 8 to 10%;
2) reduce income distribution between urban and rural populations;
3) protect the environment;
4) improve social equity (sounds almost democratic, doesn't it?).

China needs 15 million jobs annually to maintain a 10% growth rate.

Though the state still favors state-owned enterprises and it accepts the corruption and lack of competition they practice, the private enterprises also do a lot of foreign trade. The banking system in China monitors and controls transactions. Foreign trade is supervised by the Ministry of Commerce, Customs, and the Bank of China which gives businesses access to foreign currency because imports are 30% of GDP and businesses can deal directly with foreign firms.

In 2009, the Peoples Congress had the state ease credit for mortgages and lower taxes on real estate to provide more affordable housing. The state built and spent on railroads, roads, and ports to expand commerce (in 2012 public revenues were estimated at 1.8 trillion dollars and expenses at 2 trillion dollars). In 2010, wages were rising and in 2013 a minimum wage law (affecting even state-owned businesses) was passed, to be phased in by 2015 and which sets the minimum at 40% of an average urban worker's salary. And in 2010, the state owned 20.8% of U.S. Treasuries (securities).

In 2012, China's actual growth rate was 7.8%. In China, 33% of what is produced is by foreign companies producing domestically (compared to 20% in the U.S. and 25% in the European Union). By 2006, 80% of the world's computers were assembled in China with all the electronic parts imported into China as well as almost 100% of the global output of nickel, copper, and aluminum, and 45% of oil.

With a labor force of three-quarters of a billion people, in 2012 the unemployment rate was 4.1% and the inflation rate was 2.5%. In 2015, China will face a rapidly ageing population and the problem of retirement. People in China invest 50% of their savings to try and provide for then. The average gross salary in 2010 was $457 a month. Even though it is estimated to have increased to $1284 a month in 2012, future challenges await. The state has concentrated on infrastructure in order to open up the interior of the country to development since the coastal areas are where the population and industries are predominant. The three main rivers are in the south and water has to be brought up north. The power grids have been opening coal-fired plants to provide electricity and Beijing, the capital, has smog weeks where the visibility is zero or a little above. Land speculation is still ongoing with too many apartment buildings being built and no occupants to live in them. There still are factory dormitories housing 2,000 to 5,000 workers in high-rises and the work week is six days a week. Wall Street figures that maybe by 2017 but definitely by 2020 China will be the number one economy in the world.

What happened in China in 2009 gives us a better picture of economic disaster in individual savings for the Asian, European, and American economies. When Deng Xiaoping in 1980 encouraged private enterprise, small and medium size businesses sprang up and flourished. Since China doesn't have a pension or retirement system, the people try to save 50% of their earnings towards their old age, even though reverence for elders prompts children to look after their parents as they age. The trend toward urbanization is breaking down that reverential system as the young have to deal with increased costs as well as the elderly. But the entrepreneurs who succeeded in business saved up substantial sums and in 2009, when the Bank of China offered credit default swaps based on home mortgages of European and American properties with insured principal denominated in equal currencies, the offers were too good to ignore. The owners of those small and medium size businesses were allowed and encouraged to invest heavily in those swaps which seemed a good bet to people accustomed to betting on risk.

The swaps seemed a sure bet. If some of the mortgages failed, the majority would prove profitable. To people for whom home failures were considered non-existent, there could be no better bet to guarantee substantial returns on investments. When failure came and angry questions were asked, the answer was the backer of the deal was insolvent and couldn't pay off because the bets were based on the principal and the principal was backed by the guarantor and the guarantor didn't have the capital. The party or parties selling the swaps were only intermediaries and made their profits on the fees charged to buy into the swaps so only the insurer or guarantor of the swaps was responsible and if the guarantor or bondholder was bankrupt or nearly so, the loss to the buyer was total. So nobody was to blame, the investors were fleeced out of their savings, the negotiators or sellers were to be held innocent, and the instruments were worthless because somebody had to lose money for betting on the deal. It was like the savings and loan fiasco with the junk bonds combined with Wall Street's shorts and longs thrown in with a time element to make the deal complex and no regulation to answer for it.

Today, the banks themselves are the players in a market where 80% of the derivatives are interest rate swaps contracts; low bond yields are encouraging complex derivatives investments in which capital requirements are ignored and fees and risks are not fully disclosed. Yawning holes in balance sheets are or will be covered up when the investments go awry. And who is the suspect for the bailout of the institutions failing? It will again be the government.

There is a group of legislators in government who believe that the derivatives are insurance policies that the institutions use to cover their losses since 90% of those institutions' profits come from credit debt instruments and other such investment products. These legislators consider the derivatives as side bets on happenings such as companies going bankrupt and countries failing to pay their debts. They ignored the cheating when the interbank rate manipulation (or Libor scandal) was uncovered, treating it as a foreign occurrence disconnected from our banking system and don't seem aware of the determinations committee of the International Swaps and Derivatives Association which defines when a swap pays out. These ten or fifteen major banks are the exclusive members in the swaps game wherein one party makes money on a transaction and another loses money, dealing in currency swaps, interest rate swaps, and stock futures.

Whether we trust the legislators or not to look out for the welfare of the taxpayers, they may someday in the near future be some of the ones voting on another possible bailout of the financial system. It may come about this way: one early morning, about four or five by the clock, there are calls to five or six executives of the major banks and four or five calls to hedge fund managers. The callers are executives of other banks and hedge funds who have received the unfortunate news of bets gone very awry.

In 2007, there seemed to be a close partnership between Wall Street, the banks, and government. The Feds were involved in the housing business because Fannie Mae and Freddie Mac backed most of the mortgages. The banks and their subsidiaries were offering the too-good-to-be-true mortgages (or subprime) to many unqualified buyers. Wall Street fund managers, the banks, and some insurance companies were selling these bundled mortgages as assured investments (barely insured).

When the mortgages started going bad because the buyers could no longer meet the payments, Wall Street began a campaign with the failure of two investment firms who had exceeded their capital requirements (which was a favored practice then and now) to declare a financial crisis that would be greater than the Great Depression and the only way to steer clear of it would be by a government bailout.

The chief players in the swaps market (where the action involved Credit Default Obligations) asked government to take on a 5% stake in a 14 Trillion Dollar deal to rescue them from loss (p. 447 in Too Big To Fail). The amount to be distributed to them, rather than to their customers or depositors, would only be 700 Billion Dollars and the Federal Government would take on a 10 Trillion Dollar Debt, which could be handled by the taxpayers over the years.

Using the debt as collateral, the Federal Government had to borrow from other countries to cover its operating budget and those borrowings added to the debt until the tax revenues were sufficient to meet the budget. Because of its good credit record, the Federal Government could again be called on for rescue, in the thinking of the risk-takers.

This time, the sleepy-eyed financiers might be surprised by dreaded but unprepared for events. Labor in the factories and mines worldwide might realize that their terrible working conditions could only be resolved by destroying the factories and mines they worked in since the owners refused to improve working conditions and the workers saw that suicides and work stoppages weren't bringing on reforms. The swaps covering company defaults and keeping currencies proportional to company profits and output went out of control and the algorithms governing the balance of possible and impossible went haywire.

As the number of units in the categories grew negative, the multipliers of losses zoomed to embarrassing double digits and the totals of the losses far exceeded the principals of the bond guarantees. The traders glumly reported the results, admitting to themselves that bonuses would not be forthcoming but hoping to remain employed. When the committee for the payment of the swaps saw the totals, the members thought the computers had malfunctioned, some glitches must have resulted from rogue programs. After all, these were not unusual three month swaps. They were heavily bet upon because they guarded against excesses in more fluctuating areas of economies. And who could have imagined the workers coming up with these drastic actions to spite their economic conditions?

The payout called for 500 Trillion Dollars. The winning bets clamored for immediate payment to not only meet their quarterly obligations but to cover any losses in highly volatile markets. The losers knew they had to do another sell-job to the Federal Reserve and the government because in no way could they come up with that kind of money. But could the same scheme work twice? It would still be up to Congress to approve it. The House of Representatives controls the purse strings and no protections are being considered to regulate the financial markets.

Well, you say, we don't have to worry about the international markets. We have the Federal Reserve protecting our banks and the Treasury here. Surprise! Thirteen "Two Big to Fail" banks, which are members of the International Swaps and Derivatives Association, and many are American banks, were charged by the European Union with anti-competitive activity because they are preventing certain other financial institutions (namely, Deutsch Boerse and the Chicago Mercantile Exchange) from membership in the ISDA, whose members are Goldman Sachs, Citigroup, Bank of America-Merrill Lynch, Barclays, Bear Sterns, BNP Paribas, Morgan Stanley, Credit Suisse, Deutsche Bank,

HSBC, J.P. Morgan, UBS, RBS, all of whom play with the Euribor and Libor rates, which affect financial contracts such as credit cards, CDs, and derivatives. These members admit to only 13 Trillion Dollars in transactions so far in 2013 in a market reputed to deal in 600 Trillion Dollars in transactions. Now, why is the European Union sticking its nose into a closed market? Why ask, when most of the countries in the Union are practicing monetary penitence as a result of the financial crash of 2007-2008? Because the countries are at the beck and call of the bankers. True, the Union and U.S. are trying to control any cross-border SWAPS that are transacted but that doesn't open up the market to financial information on the part of the members. Every financial instrument, including currency, is at the mercy of the banks and the brokers of financial dealings. Why worry, you say, since the market seems to be taking care of itself perfectly well? If it wants to exclude candidates for membership that it doesn't approve of, well then, isn't it policing itself the way it should? The problem is more than letting in or out more members. The problem is the current members aren't affirming that any debts will be handled internally. It's bad enough they're gambling with their customers' money, but, if a group of them are losers and exceed their capital reserves, should governments (taxpayers) have to bail them out? The ISDA plays winners and losers in betting on financial dealings where some win and others lose and one must wonder if they manipulate to balance the winners and losers but one thing they can't manipulate is the capitalization of each member. Both the EU and the IMF and the U.S. Federal Reserve and the Treasury are trying to make the banks increase their capitalizations to the point of what is thought to be one step away from catastrophic disaster but in a market where all the money in the world is played with, and beyond, disaster is only a guess as well as a nightmare to be avoided. Consider that the EU and IMF think in terms of billions of euros whereas the U.S. is trillions of dollars in debt and the governments in the world have been hoodwinked into buying into banks in order to guarantee interbank lending on an international level.

How did this come about? The U.S. government answered the cries of the bankers when they first contacted the Treasury Secretary who notified the Federal Reserve Chairman that the Treasury didn't have the actual cash to prevent a disaster in the billions of dollars, which was misjudged because the market ran into trillions of dollars since nobody had sat down to total the amounts until a figure was needed to perform a bailout of the financial institutions. The bailout was an underpinning of the financial system: the government would assume the debt, the Treasury would furnish 700 Billion Dollars to a select list of financial institutions, and the financial instruments would take the loss by losing value. In order for the government to take on the debt and approve the bailout, the leader of the House of Representatives had to be convinced of the gravity of the situation and the need for quick action and a vote of approval. The President, Vice President, and the Senate were told of what the House needed to do and the need for their confirmation and lobbying of the members for quick approval to avoid utter collapse. Within eight months of financial disaster, the bailout was done, the debt assumed, the Treasury with a pile of money transfers, and the politicians patting each other on the back as they crossed their fingers for luck in the upcoming elections.

For years afterwards, the financial instruments were many times in the news as answers and actions were sought to remedy the problems. The Treasury was paid back by the outfits that had been loaned the money during the crisis, but, instead of applying the surplus to the national debt, the Treasury is sitting on it in case of another crisis, supposedly. The Federal Reserve is trying to figure out a way to energize the national economy while advising the banks to increase their capital reserves (while letting the SWAPS market self-regulate itself and ignore the use of the depositors' money as collateral for bets). The House of Representatives complains about the Dodd-Frank law while limiting the number of regulators and wondering why the regulators aren't policing interbank lending deals. Wall Street is comfortable with its cash and wants more, having gotten government to allow hedge funds to advertise for investors. The "Too Big to Fail" banks figure that since they got billions for the last crisis, it shouldn't be too difficult to get, maybe not 500 Trillion Dollars, but 5 Trillion Dollars next time.

The rest of the world is doing things differently.

As World War Two was being fought, twenty-nine countries in 1944 met at Bretton Woods in England to discuss how to reconstruct the world's international payment system. Since that conference in 1945, the International Monetary Fund was created and we now have its headquarters in Washington, D.C. and a balance of payments system for 188 member countries to oversee their international monetary and financial systems and their economic and financial policies.

Based on a quota system, the countries contribute money to a financial pool so that deficit countries can borrow funds temporarily. Since 1950 to the present, the Fund uses a Rapid Financing Instrument to furnish emergency assistance to members facing urgent balance of payment needs.

Even today, those Americans who advocate a return to the gold standard roundly criticize President Nixon of the U.S. for taking the country off of gold, but in 1971 the IMF countries went off floating exchange rates in order to oversee fixed exchange rates between countries. As a result of going to fixed exchange rates, the IMF now manages not just exchange rates but also the economic policy of countries as well as providing short-term capital to aid balance of payments.

The IMF doesn't require collateral for loans but requires the country seeking help to do policy reform. If the country does not reform, then the IMF can withhold the funds needed. To enforce repayment, the country that obtained help must meet certain conditions to restructure itself and improve its financial condition. This structured adjustment might require a country: to practice austerity; to export products; to devalue its currency; to lift trade restrictions; to open domestic stock markets to supplement foreign direct investment; to balance budgets; to remove price controls and state subsidies; to privatize state-owned businesses; to put in place national laws guaranteeing the rights of foreign investors; to fight corruption and enhance governing. The condition of a member in the IMF is more important than the collection of money for a loan.

Since 1995, as a result of instituting a General Data Dissemination System and a Special Dissemination System, the information gleaned has shown that reducing government services results in increases in unemployment, and the lowering of taxes increases budget deficits. Further, loaning out money by itself has to be accompanied by reforms, otherwise corrections will never be forthcoming and the debt will increase to the detriment of not only that country but to the harm of others as well.

The IMF itself is not without criticisms. Many disparagers hold it to be out of touch with citizens, cultures, and local economic conditions of both world and third-world countries. They also point out how the IMF advises belt-tightening to a country with no belt, like many African countries. For all the complaints, the riposte is who or what else is the watchdog for financial doings between countries? The United Nations deals with the political doings between countries of the world. But when it comes to money changing hands around the world, the matter is even more delicate than politics. A case in point is a speech by the Deputy Managing Director of the IMF, Naoyuki Shinohara in June of 2013, in which he tries to deal with the problem of derivatives and their effects on world finances and economies. He calls for controlling their use by watching out for the availability of credit on the part of the banks and their handling of the money supply as furnished by depositors, to see whether the banks are firming up businesses by providing them with the means to get the production of goods and services going and flowing. The United States of America, the United Kingdom, France, Germany, China, Russia, and Japan are members of the IMF along with 181 other countries.

The four currencies used in the SWAPS market are the U.S. dollar, the British pound, the euro, and the Japanese yen. As of March 2013, there are 70 registered swaps dealers worldwide. According to ISDA estimates, swaps contracts totaled 62 trillion dollars from 2000 to 2007. The Depository Trust and Clearing Corporation states that in the first half of 2013 the swaps contracts have totaled to 24 trillion dollars and the swaps used by investors speculate on companies' and governments' ability to repay their debts. Credit swaps pay a buyer face value if a borrower fails to meet its obligation, less the value of the defaulted debt. Investors typically spread their swap trading among several dealers rather than one, but generally only one clearinghouse is used. The swaps contracts deal in notional value so no actual cash changes hands but rather there are payment flows, meaning everything being dealt is on account.

The stock markets of the world are fascinated by the games and tactics the hedge funds and banks come out with. For instance, when the residential mortgage contracts were being sold, Goldman Sachs took lower liability, discounting their upfront payment by using the Overnight Indexed Swaps rate (OIS) instead of the bigger liability LIBOR rate by using a countering bank (which got a handling fee), which SWAP paid off a higher profit in winning due to the higher valuation in basis points for the high risk, and, since the countering bank was using euros, Goldman Sachs took the profit in dollars which gave a higher profit return. Using the LIBOR rate would have given Goldman Sachs only a 60 basis point return, whereas the OIS rate gave Goldman a 344 basis point return, e.g. a five year interest rate swap of 100 million dollars, at present value of 10 million dollars, would only be two million dollars at the OIS discount rate, and, if paid in euros would be ostensibly more than dollars, but the payoff in dollars would be a higher value return (Matt Cameron in Risk Magazine, May 2013).

The world's largest interest rate swaps clearinghouse is London based LCH Clearnet, which handled 22 trillion dollars of the 24 trillion dollars swap contracts (Leising and Brush, Bloomberg News, March 2013). The market is growing bigger and the risks are becoming greater. To realize how big, let's consider the European Union and some of the countries in it.

If you traveled in Europe in the 1980s, you might have been inconvenienced at every border crossing by having to show your passport and answer your purpose for visiting that particular country. The chunnel between England and France could have been delayed many years more were it not for the Maastricht Treaty in 1993 which established the European Union. The aim of the Union was to ensure free movement of people, goods, services, and capital among its members. It has 28 member countries and has a Parliament elected every five years by the European Union citizens. Its combined population numbers 500 million people which is 7.3% of the world's population and its nominal gross domestic product (GDP) is 16.5 trillion dollars which is 20% of the world's GDP. People can move between countries without a passport.

Earlier, in 1989, a monetary union was conceived, an eurozone, which was noted in the Maastricht Treaty and was to be implemented as a currency union by 1999. The currency exchange system began as the European Monetary Institute but in June of 1998 was succeeded by the European Central Bank (ECB) with a fixed rate exchange system. When a recession developed in the United Kingdom as a result of a trade imbalance, the UK had to withdraw from the ECB as the pound sterling fell, and that country has been on a floating rate system since.

The currency of the ECB is the euro, which began in January of 1999 and was circulated by the 17 member countries which use it in 2002. The method of implementing the new coinage and paper was very practical. Each household in every member country was provided with a pouch containing a couple hundred euros of the new coins and paper so that as the citizens shopped in the coming months the new currency would circulate and the old would revert to the banks from the merchants with the old being taken out of circulation.

Even billionaires are greedy. The problem with money is it's never enough. The grass is always greener on the other side of the fence, we always say. In the U.S., the Federal Reserve has set up regional governors to oversee banks. Their strategic placement and periodic board meetings would suggest close regulatory supervision but they are treated by politicians and banks more as solons. During the banking crisis of 2007-8, we heard of the Treasury Secretary, the Federal Reserve Chairman, and Congress acting to treat the crisis but no word of the governors, outside of Timothy Geitner, being involved.

Most financial writers and economists agree that the U.S. subprime mortgage crisis caused the worldwide financial crisis. Banks in Iceland, Norway, Sweden, and Denmark as well as banks in Asia and Africa were involved and experienced financial hardships. In Europe, the leaders of the European Central Bank came up with a Bank Rescue Plan in 2008 in which the governments of the European Union would buy into the banks to boost their finances and guarantee interbank lending, almost like in the U.S. where the Federal Reserve got the government to bailout the banks because a precedent had been set at the time of the Savings and Loan Crisis in the 1980s and in the 1990s with interstate branching.

The European Central Bank injected 500 billion euros into its member banks in June of 2009 to keep poorer performing economies from hurting larger ones. The Treaty of Lisbon added an amendment to the original European Union constitution to allow this injection. Back in the 1990s, when the European Union was first being formed, politics brought in Greece and Italy, even though they had debt higher than 60% of their GDPs, their budget deficits were higher than 30% of their GDPs, and their interest rates were higher than European Union averages. Because Greece was a big problem that even the mechanics of a temporary bailout couldn't solve, and, even though the ECB bought Greek and Italian bonds to prevent a bailout later, there was a need to keep financial stability in the EU. The Treaty of Lisbon called for an European Stability Mechanism, to be headquartered in Luxembourg, to be begun in October of 2012 that would be an international financial institution set up by the euro area countries to provide financial assistance to its members to safeguard financial stability.

In 2013, the European Stability Mechanism did takeover, teaming up with funds from the IMF to provide a temporary bailout mechanism to stabilize the Greek problem. The European Stability Mechanism (ESM) was empowered to grant loans to its members; it can provide precautionary financial assistance; it can purchase bonds of beneficiary members in primary and secondary markets; it can finance recapitalization of financial institutions through loans to governments.

Proposed for the second half of 2014 is what is called a Single Supervisory Mechanism, a way to recapitalize the member banks. The plan is to have a fund with maximum capacity of a half a trillion euros and a total capital of a hundred billion euros with a beginning fund of eighty billion euros paid in by the end of 2014 with the rest in callable capital. If a bank requests funds, the funds will be paid only upon agreement by a Board of Governors.

What really is being sought for the eurozone is an European Fiscal Union (EFU). Unfortunately, the national parliaments are slow to draft a treaty enabling such and the member countries are not enthusiastic about approving participation in an EFU. Is it any wonder that the member countries can't come to ratify a treaty? The past is riddled with political moves to just embarrass some countries that many members wanted to deny funds to because they had overspent their budgets and were excusing their excesses so as not to injure their citizens economically. There is a dilemma here.

Wall Street says the European banks are sitting on a lot of money and if they don't start to loan it out, they could cause a deflation. The European governments are trying to eliminate the deficits of many of the EU countries to get trade and economies going again by having the ECB and IMF loan euros to bring accounts into balance. This has been taking place from 2011 through 2013. As their GDPs continue to fall, the European governments see the unemployment continue to rise. The American economists are split, whether the U.S. labor force has structural unemployment or cyclical unemployment. Structural unemployment is when jobs go out of existence because the economy changes. These changes can be improvements in production, different demographics, relocation of facilities, wage levels inconsistent with actual cost of living and living standards, and changing age levels. Cyclical unemployment is when there is a pause in the economy to account for delays in money supply or production. The U.S. and European unemployment seem to be more the result of structural changes due to technological advances but statistics hint at changes in age levels.

Many young people are unemployed or employed in low wage jobs. Many low level and mid-level managers earn considerably less than the salaries of pre-2008. Supervisors have no time for training because they have to maintain a level of production set by computerized goal-setting projections. Competency of employees has fallen to less than a fifth of the work force. Stagnation is creeping into the work forces because human motivation based on grit, determination, and achievement is not encouraged. Disbelieving that competence comes from being on the job longer, employers were quick to rid themselves of older workers.

When 2007-2008 came along, most employers, both in the U.S. and Europe, encouraged their older workers to retire or eliminated their jobs outright, realizing a substantial cost-saving of doing business. Over 50% of the pension money for these workers was invested by the banks and governments into the derivatives market because everyone thought the housing values in the U.S. and some European countries were sure bets inasmuch as housing was an area of economies that was solid. People didn't want to lose their homes. Shelter is a prime requirement for good healthy living and safe and secure investment.

That was in the past. When the bondholders of the institutions involved in the mortgages started to lose money and couldn't back up the defaults, the financial collapse hurt the homeowners, the banks, the governments, and many millionaire investors. The ones who seem to have prospered are the hedge funds, the investment banks, and the very wealthy. Many older workers saw their nest eggs reduced at least a third, their home mortgages threatened by foreclosure and very few job openings for older workers. This tremendous loss of income and savings for seniors has not really been acknowledged by economists. The money of seniors has been treated as inheritances to be passed on to future generations or to provide for healthcare in advanced old age. Because of modern medicine and careful attention to living habits, seniors are experiencing longer life spans, more active lifestyles, and helping raise their grandchildren by covering expenses and many times providing housing and necessities for their adult children. Pilfering the seniors' savings and pensions by fraudulent schemes, the politicians and investment bankers have upset economies and financial markets and caused living standards to decline or remain stagnant for much of the world's population.

Every country is different. We tend to identify people by the country they're from, rather than thinking of everybody as earthlings. Many countries contributed to the building of the space station but now there seems to be only one way to get there and back. Is our fascination with space because we think there might be other beings on another planet or because we fear that someday a large chunk of rock will come hurtling out of the sky and smash earth to pieces so we might as well try to find another planet to start a colony? If we can't live together on this earth, how will we survive together someplace else? Just look at how other countries do things. The European Union tries to let its member countries operate independently, but in money matters it wants to have a say in policy making.

In the 1990s, the young students in the colleges and universities in Ireland took a liking to computers and many studied programming. The wages in Ireland were low, even for college graduates. Many didn't want to leave the country but making a living was difficult in a country noted for strife and not many jobs. All that changed when the banks and investment companies started what came to be called financial centers. The fever that struck Americans in 1929 came back in 1989 and went worldwide from then on.

Everybody can get rich quick if you invest your money instead of letting it lay around fever tampered with the minds of anyone with a nest egg or a couple of thousand or more in cash or in a bank account earning a paltry much less than five percent. Sellers of financial instruments could send your money to any country you wanted, or where taxes would be lower or returns would be higher. Send your money to Ireland where those smart young people know how to run those complicated money-making machines, the financial brokers and sellers advised.

The money came pouring in. By 2008, the capital invested in Irish banks was 80% from the United Kingdom, 13% from the U.S., 5% from off-shore funding, and 2% from the euro zone. All those young college graduates felt secure enough to get married, start a family, and buy a house in Ireland. The Irish banks recycled the money coming in by putting it into property loans. The real estate prices went up because all those young families in Ireland wanted a home of their own and had good jobs providing them with the promise of future earnings to cover the costs. Only so much property was available so no new property deals exposed the fragile cash-flows of developers and revealed the high prices of property causing developers and buyers rushing to withdraw money or obtain loans. The banks didn't have enough money to cover withdrawals or to handle loans or to cover the deposits and pay interest so the loans started declining and deposits were growing greater than the capital the banks needed to operate safely. The six Irish banks, with loans declining and deposits greater than their assets, needed major cash injections.

The government in Dublin bailed out the two largest Irish banks (Allied Irish Bank and Bank of Ireland) to the tune of 3.5 billion euros each and nationalized the Anglo Irish Bank in 2008 because of hidden loans exceeding assets. The European Union, through the European Financial Stability Facility, and the International Monetary Fund guaranteed and approved the state aid. Everything was blamed on an overheated economy, price inflation, and chicanery by bank officials and state regulators.

An Indiana University study in November 2010 put the Irish debt at 85 billion euros but by August 2011 total funding for the six Irish banks by the European Central Bank and the Irish Central Bank came to about 150 billion euros. Once the corrupt bank officials and state regulators were out of the way and prosecuted, and the Irish government had paid out one and a half billion euros in April 2012 (and another one billion euros in October 2012) to unsecured bank bondholders, and the homeowners continued to pay on their mortgages, control and responsibility appeared to be coming back to the Irish economy but austerity was still demanded by the government and the European Union since newer EU states like Estonia, Croatia, and Latvia continued to press for membership. In the meantime, property taxes remain extremely high in Ireland.

The only thing Greece has in common with Ireland is sky-high property taxes. Ireland had its potato famine; Greece has been blessed with olives, fish, and cheese. The paradox of Greece is how can a country with so much money be so poor? It is held that corruption and lying are Greece's number one problem. The country took on the euro in 2001, but only on paper, until 2009 when they used the actual money. In 2011, 63% of the people favored keeping the euro. Greece has more money than all the Balkan states combined. And the Greek banks seem to open a new bank everyday in the Balkans. The Hellenic Greek Bank, together with the rest of the Greek banks and the Greek banks in the southern half of Cyprus, have over a half trillion euros in assets (the northern half of Cyprus uses the Turkish lira). The Greeks don't get along with the Macedonians but Macedonia is one of Greece's big trading partners and Greece loans money to it.

Greece has the second largest maritime fleet, after Japan. Thirty-three million barrels of crude oil are imported into Greece and thirty-eight million barrels of refined oil are exported (the Greek oil wells only produce one and half million barrels of crude). Russia is the number one importer to Greece and Turkey is the number one exporter from Greece. Only 7% of the Greek population is employed in the export business, however, with service industries employing 85%, manufacturing 4%, and electronics 3%. Because of the austerity program imposed on Greece by the European Union, 27% of the overall population is unemployed but 64% of the youths are unemployed. With much import and export going on, Greece finds itself as a middleman, with little employment to provide for a budget which spends 31% of its funds on pensions, healthcare and its form of social security (6 billion euros for pensions, twenty-two billion euros for healthcare and social security). Another reason for the hard times is because shipping is way down. Pipelines are moving a lot more oil and people aren't buying many goods with so much unemployment in the land. The banks have a lot of money but the government doesn't because of the slow economy and the debt caused by the low employment. The money brokers keep hoping Greece will drop the euro and go back to the drachma (the exchange rate would become 340 drachmas to the euro). The only people that would help would be the money speculators.

What good has austerity done for Greece? It has made the rich richer and half of the businesses are not paying taxes. Worldwide, it seems that venture capital firms either didn't risk very much of their richest clients' funds in the home mortgage fiasco, or that the derivatives invested in turned out to be the ones that paid off handsomely when the defaults occurred. The businesses either avoid paying taxes or declare that business activity is so negative that there are pitiful earnings and no profits.

Greece is one of the countries that pays insurance companies to provide healthcare to its citizens. Because of austerity, the government has cut healthcare, so many physicians are breaking the law (which says no healthcare provided for indigents without insurance, instead of saying the government won't pay the bills for healthcare) by continuing to treat seriously ill patients (like with cancer) on their own. Hoping that the churches and relief agencies will provide food and shelter to the poor (foreclosures have thrown 70,000 into the homeless ranks), the politicians don't seem to realize that the congregations are hurting economically as well and can't provide assistance.

The emergency funds the IMF and ECB provide the Greek government do not provide relief or strengthen the economy. The money gained by austerity is going to pay off the country's debt so the loans made to the country are just filling in the holes caused by the austerity (and not filling in the holes completely) and the economy continues to weaken because there are no resources to improve trade, maintain the infrastructure, and provide employment.

Is there a solution better than austerity? Yes, but it means the Greek government would have to shake some of those half trillion euros the Greek banks have in assets to loan the government at something like a half to one percent annual interest rate over thirty years to pay off the deficits, loan the citizens six months of living expenses, and pass laws, in case of banks' intransigence to the deal, to tax them for some of those excess profits for the next five years. Unfortunately, the IMF has not fared well in encouraging banks, even worldwide, to work closer with the regulators and allow credit and loans to the business communities, let alone the governments, in order to have trade and the economies to flourish.

In the meantime, a prodigal daughter of the European Union sits with a glut of housing with no hope in sight for a resurgence of sales and a return to prosperity. Spain has an inventory of two million homes waiting to be sold. Housing accounts for 10% of Spain's economy. At least eight hundred thousand houses are used homes and seven hundred thousand are completed construction but no sales. Over four hundred thousand Britons live on the coast or own homes in Spain.

Besides the British, there has been a huge immigration from Africa and other European countries up until 2011, and even since; many immigrants may have moved away but still keep their properties in Spain in hopes of a grand recovery. Ninety-eight per cent of the home loans are priced off of the EURIBOR rates. Properties in foreclosure or foreclosed on total 450,000 and the unemployment rate as of May 2013 was 26% (Mail Online News, July, 2013). The average net salary in Spain is 18,679 euros ($24,293). When employed, 70% of the workforce is in services, 14% in industry, 10% in construction, 4.5% in agriculture, fishing, and farming. Total workforce is 22.9 million people. What is meant by services is really domestics, who have helped the economy keep on somewhat of an even keel. Granted that the national debt is $2.1 Trillion (June 2010) but the country has a 248 billion euros trade surplus even though imports total 270 billion euros. The three economic backbone regions of the country's economy are Valencia, Murcia, and Catalonia. They support the export market of machinery, motor vehicles, chemicals, shipbuilding, foodstuffs, electronic devices, and pharmaceuticals.

Spain imports from Germany, France, Italy, China, the Netherlands, and the United Kingdom. It imports fuel, chemicals, consumer goods, and machinery. It exports to France, Germany, Italy, Portugal, and the United Kingdom.

Whether it's because of the large influx of immigrants or the recession of the early 1990s, Spain is not noted for its education, which is contrary to the glory of the Alhambra of the Moors back in the 15th and 16th centuries when Spain was a world power and algebra and trigonometry were introduced into western learning while Ferdinand and Isabella not only funded Christopher Columbus but expended much of the country's wealth on military endeavors.

In the twentieth century, the Spanish Civil War so weakened the country that during the Second World War it was treated as a vassal of Germany rather than as a neutral country, though it was considered a refuge by many people escaping Hitler's persecutions in the rest of Europe.

Spain is Europe's California – a nice place to visit but hard to make a living in. That changed without fanfare after the recession ended in 1993 and American and European manufacturers saw how easy it was to do business internationally. Like what was said about job interviewing in American companies with international team members wherein so many companies do not take into account the cultural differences of the team, so too in the romance countries where the lady of the house has a say in her husband's business, the American companies tried to bulldoze foreign firms by telling them how to run their businesses. Were it not for the foreign banks and the IMF (through its data studies in the mid to late 1990s comparing policy initiatives that contribute to business success), the American firms trying to do business internationally would have failed to interest foreign firms and investors. The American companies had earlier done a very clever thing. They had sent consultants – experienced machinists, shop supervisors, and production troubleshooters- to shops and factories that would be doing work for American firms or becoming partners with American firms, to improve their production techniques and improve quality control so waste was minimized and production increased, leading to higher profits for the firms and partners.

Instead of letting the economy work its way into paying off the nation's debt by encouraging business to maintain exports (Spain is South America's second largest exporter), encouraging tourism by eliminating the tax on pensions and social security so immigrants could come in and buy up the excess housing inventory, the government borrowed euros from the Social Security fund to back up the Spanish bonds offered to private investors, taxed and cut payments to the recipients of pensions and Social Security so that seniors fell into the poverty level or close to it, and increased taxes on the general population as part of an austerity program to lower the debt by 2015 to 2.5% of GDP. The only purpose of these drastic steps was to make Spanish debt attractive to investors. These steps were taken by Argentina in the 2000s. It's called robbing the piggy bank legally and making seniors suffer because they have no recourse to jobs or other income. Ireland and Spain are notable examples of this. If the bonds are not attractive to outside investors, then the Social Security Reserve Funds become the buyer of the bonds. Ninety per cent of the 65 billion euros ($85.7 Billion) in the fund has been invested in the Spanish debt.

Can the seniors in Spain fight back? They are fearful of more foreclosures and, like in Greece, of continuing austerity. If they organize like the seniors in Argentina, where ports were shut down and buildings closed, or, as in the U.S. where AARP has a strong lobby in government, then the government in Spain has to listen and stimulate the economy instead of cutting taxes for the wealthy.

In Portugal, where over a third of the population is seniors, the government has reduced pensions, is taxing pensions and Social Security, cutting funds for education and health care, and 87% of the retirees are getting less than 611 euros ($794) a month, making 77% of the seniors not being able to cover basic costs (Coimbra University, Economic and Social Council). The politicians excuse for these steps is that the European Union requires a debt ceiling of 3% GDP or less and since the ECB and IMF bailed out Portugal in 2010 because of a 78 billion euros deficit in the budget and 18% unemployment (Christian Science Monitor by Andrea Cala, June 27, 2013) out of a labor force of 5.48 million, these austerity measures were necessary in a country with wages and bonuses of public servants and the costs of public works inflated enough to max out the interest rate to 7% on ten year government bonds and too much deficit. True, public servants' wages were cut and tax increases added to payrolls but Portugal is considered a high income developed country with revenues of 94.6 billion dollars and expenses of 107.4 billion dollars (Wikipedia 2012). There are two reasons for this imbalance. First, because four huge international exporting companies send paper and paper products, wood panels, cork (one third of Portugal is covered by forests), and canned fish worldwide, and the average gross salary in Portugal is 894 euros ($1,300) a month (Wikipedia 2010). Second, in 1974, over a million people from the African colonies came back to Portugal and caused economic problems by stretching resources in education, employment, and manufacturing. The Socialist Party says that the austerity imposed on Portugal goes to pay off international creditors. Here, too, the seniors are suffering and need to organize to stop this payoff to private investors and have a say in government.

As you sit at table, enjoying a delicious pasta dinner, accompanied by a bottle of Chianti, you find it hard to understand the economic difficulties you hear about Italy, the ninth largest economy in the world, the fifth largest in Europe, and the second largest producer of wines in the world. You can't forget that the rifle that helped kill President John F. Kennedy was made in Italy, that the Maserati you'd like to have and be able to wear your Armani suit in, are all products of Italy, just like the Pirelli tires on your present car.

You hear that the unemployment rate in Italy is 8.5% and the young adults' rate is 27%. The unions are so strong that seniors are protected by laws, making them hard to fire, but the young adults have only short term contracts for work so they have to hop from job to job and pay high taxes. Because the ECB loaned some 20 billion euros to the Italian government in 2010, the budget deficit for 2012 was 2.7% and the Italian bonds interest rate jumped to 6.74% in November 2011 (though it dropped to 5% in February 2012) which frightens investors because anything close to 7% rate means no return on an initial investment unless you're willing to wait 20 years in hopes that the premium on the bond by then will have weathered inflation and its value restored.

People in Italy pay 45% more than the rest of Europe for their electricity. Yet Italy is one of the biggest solar, wind, and hydro electricity generators. The Italians, though, because of the Chernobyl disaster, closed all their nuclear generating plants and import electricity from France where nuclear power plants abound.

The biggest chunk of public debt is owned by the wealthy who live in Italy. There are many billionaires and just to throw out some names, recognize Ferrari, Armani, Prada, Benetton, Agnelli, Berlusconi? They are, as we say, filthy rich with high levels of savings but low levels of personal debt. If you missed the 60 Minutes TV show on Luxottica, they are almost a worldwide monopoly in eyeglasses and optical products (brands such as RayBan, Bausch and Lomb, LensCrafters, Pearle Vision, and EyeMed, the second largest vision benefits company in the U.S.) (Wikipedia 2013).

Italy also does business with its largest trading partners: Germany (12%), France (11%), Spain (7%). So are there two Italys? Yes. Besides the islands of Sardinia and Sicily, there is the north of Italy with the industrial triangle of Milan, Turin, and Genoa (second busiest port in the Mediterranean after Marseilles) and a high GDP; then there is the south of Italy with a low GDP, high unemployment, and corruption (both political and mafia: small and medium size companies involved in retail and agriculture who have to pay for protection).

The government rescued the banks who lost money in the 2008 worldwide fiasco but now the government has a lot of debt and the banks won't give credit so businesses can't expand or modernize (speaking of the businesses in the south of Italy). The big question is – can the better half of the country make up for the lesser half until that half makes a comeback and the whole country can then move ahead? Only time will tell.

Seventy-eight per cent of electricity in France is generated by nuclear plants. No wonder they can export it to Italy. But then, France's economy is only second to Germany in Europe. It also has the highest number of millionaires in Europe, 2.6 million of them, and is the wealthiest country in Europe and fourth wealthiest in the world. With 63 million people and a 14 trillion dollar economy, France is the world's number one tourist destination, ahead of Spain even.

With a labor force of 29.6 million people, working in services (71.8%), industry (24.3%), and agriculture (3.8%), as of March 2012 the unemployment rate was 11% and the poverty rate among the general population was 8.8%, with the average salary of a French worker being 1,712 euros ($2,396) per month as of 2006. The country's main industries are machinery, chemicals, autos, metallurgy, aircraft, electronics, textiles, food processing, and tourism. In 2012, France exported 567.5 billion dollars worth of goods and imported 658.9 billion dollars worth of machinery and equipment, vehicles, crude oil, aircraft, plastics, and chemicals. France is the second largest exporter of agricultural products after the U.S., and the fourth largest weapons exporter in the world. Some of the best known French companies are Carrefour, the world's second largest retail group; Total, the world's fourth largest oil company; Danone, the fifth largest food company and the largest mineral water company in the world. French companies invest $220 billion outside of France, being only second in the world to U.S. companies. Sixty per cent of French trade is with European Union countries (all of this information is from Wikipedia).

Whereas in the U.S. and U.K. there are mostly private companies, in France the government owns shares in companies in banking, energy production, autos, transportation, and telecommunications. As a result, the country has revenues of $1.34 trillion and expenses of $1.458 trillion (2012 est.). The government has 1.83 billion euros of debt compared to public debt of 89.9% of GDP. France is recognized as having the best health care system in the world because even though various occupations have their own contributory programs and workers have payroll deductions to cover health care, social security, and general taxes, anyone needing medical care is provided for, including indigents.

France loves its cars, Renault and Peugeot, but right now the prices are too high and exports are suffering from lower priced foreign makes. Consumers aren't spending and the government has raised taxes, 7 billion euros ($9 billion). Public debt is 90% and the tax increases are hurting the economy. France, Spain, and Greece are seeing wages and production of goods cut, and economists are saying the euro is valued too high. They are saying the euro should be priced between $1.15 and $1.20 and no higher to beat out the competition in the currency markets. Mario Draghi of the ECB says you can't lower the euro and hope to be competitive in the long run. Others say the euro is high because there is no longer a threat of an eurozone breakup and the interest rates are still tending towards the high rather than the low. With the easy money policies of the U.S., U.K., and Japan, the euro will continue to be wanted. (La Jeune Politque by Anastasia Rab, February 2013).

The French love the joy of living rather than worrying about interest rates, deficits (the French one is 4.8% of GDP in contrast to the EU's caution of no more than 3% of GDP), the slowing of exports, and keeping the euro (international trade always involves at least two national currencies). The Great Depression of the 1930s was caused by countries putting up trade barriers against each other so that world trade was made difficult. The Marshall Plan after the Second World War worked because it made countries lower or eliminate tariffs. Trade barriers to protect industries and workers do not work. When foreigners invest in the U.S., for instance, rather than just sell their goods here, the U.S. economy is better because when goods are transacted money comes out of a country, compared to capital coming into a country because of investment (USA Online.com). Is it any wonder French and U.S. companies are keeping their monies out of their own countries? Worldwide banking is taking place here and now. The problem with banks is not home and business loans. The problem is with derivatives. They are not only high risk financial instruments. They are free-ranging methods of gaining advantage by chancing that worldwide events follow outcomes dictated by mathematical formulae, rather than cautious exploration and rational decision.

There is an American Libor but it is run out of the London exchange that handles the international Libor. Even though Libor stands for London Interbank Offered Rate, the word is used to mean the rate at which the world's most preferred borrowers are able to borrow money (and some not so preferred). There are three other world markets with Libors: India, Singapore, and Hong Kong.

The rate is fixed daily by the British Bankers' Association and is derived from the filtered average of the world's most creditworthy banks' interbank deposit rates for large loans with maturities that range from overnight to one full year. The rate is set by sixteen international member banks that deal in $360 trillion financial products worldwide, along with 223 member banks representing sixty nations and thirty-seven associated professional firms. The United Kingdom controls the Libor through laws made by its Parliament.

Eighteen banks contribute to fixing the U.S. dollar Libor. In 2012 eighty per cent of the subprime mortgages were linked to the U.S. Libor and forty-five per cent of the prime adjustable rate mortgages. American municipalities borrowed around 75% of their money through financial products linked to the American Libor. Mortgage lenders and credit card agencies set their rates relative to the Libor. The International Swaps and Derivatives Association specifically references the Libor for over the counter interest rate derivatives (Investopedia, 2013).

If you're an American company doing business overseas, or an overseas company doing business in America, or in another country, you have access to a number of banks that can offer you a trustworthy interest rate for a length of time on your loan that will help you recoup your borrowings from profitable operations in markets where tariffs are falling due to the realization that you can set up your operation where the profit can be greater due to reduced costs of labor and materials and open markets where goods are more in demand. The Libors are calculated for ten currencies and were first used in financial markets in 1986. By the mid-1990s, the World Trade Organization seemed to be effective in lowering trade tariffs among better off wealthy nations, and in the early 2000s, the sharing of Information Technology was being widely disbursed, considering how much the financial changes that were occurring must have been affecting world trade, including agricultural products where arguments for and against the two methods of determining exchange, namely, price per ton and price per arranged lot, were being hotly debated between developing countries, islands, and better off wealthy countries. Manufacturing and Information Technology are doing a better job of lowering tariffs than agricultural products countries, but progress is being made and again, time will tell.

When the United Kingdom discovered oil in the North Sea in 1975, a sigh of relief and hope for drastically cutting imports rose in the country. The old refinery complex in Grangemouth, Scotland was working fine and several years later a pipeline was built to ship the refined oil to Ireland for storage until British Petroleum needed it for distribution worldwide. BP sold the refinery shortly after to INEOS, a privately owned U.K. based chemicals company when the cost of improvement might make it less competitive for worldwide markets. Fear not, in 2011, INEOS and Lavere (out of Marseilles, France) joined with the Chinese oil company, Petrochina, to form Petrolneos Company, a giant worldwide supplier. But the North Sea oil and gas production has failed to lower imports for the U.K.

The United Kingdom is still a member of the European Union but it uses the pound sterling as currency and is on a floating rate exchange system which hasn't helped it avoid low pay and few benefits for its workers (like Spain and Ireland), and its unemployment rate in third quarter 2013 was 7.7% (Denmark doesn't belong to the EU and is on a floating rate exchange system and uses its krone for currency and, like Germany, it has high tariffs, high interest rates, and stresses the quality of its own goods to lower imports and maintain mostly a local economy – there is always one exception). The Gordon Cameron government blames the previous Labour government for the woes of 2008 and since, as well as having to weather a two million immigration to the U.K. since 2008 which is blamed for pay falling 6.3% and four out of five jobs since 2010 being in the low pay sector. Nevertheless, the U.K. economy is 2.7% smaller than in 2008 which the press blames on government spending and investment (The Guardian, September 8, 2013).

Whereas Germany and China are global export champions, and the U.S. has benefited from China and the Far East buying its industrial equipment and cars (Buick is outselling its U.S. figures in China), the U.K. businesses are sitting on their cash, proven by 10% lower investing in 2012 compared to 2010. Leo Osbourne's court case against the government for freeing the derivatives business is getting only half-hearted support from the general population because 75% of the euro derivative trading is only taking place in London (The Guardian, December 2011). Curiously, the EU banks are likewise reluctant to lead, with investment abroad falling 54% compared to 2004, though foreign investment totaled $3.5 trillion in the U.S., which was down 39% from 1999 and 17% of total global investment in 2011. The problem seems to be German demands for tough enforced controls on public borrowing and spending. Germany is the austerity pusher, yet it had a 4% growth to over eleven trillion euros, mostly by exports to non-European Union countries (The Guardian, September 8, 2013).

To illustrate how adaptable Germany is to taking advantage of hard times, let's start with how Hitler was able to pay off the debt the Allies charged Germany with for the First

World War and still was able to furnish German manufacturers with the money to produce the armaments used to fight the Spanish Civil War and World War Two.

When Hjalmar Schacht (1877-1970) graduated from college, he left Germany to come to the U.S. to work in a J.P. Morgan bank in Brooklyn, New York, and was recognized as clever enough to be assigned to use a subsidiary to set up shell banks. Returning to Germany because of the Great Depression, in 1930 he ran the Bank of International Settlements to pay off the German debt to the Allies, but he made sure money was furnished to the German armament manufacturers and accomplished the most rapid decline in unemployment of any country during the Great Depression. Making friends with Hermann Goering through his social contacts, he was introduced to Adolf Hitler. When Hitler was made Chancellor of Germany in 1933, he made Schacht Reichsbank President and Economic Minister because Schacht had accomplished his economic miracle by setting up a limited liability company called MEFO (Metallurgische Forschungsgeseblschaft) which issued bills of exchange convertible into Reischmarks on demand (which were nothing more than balance sheet entities) and avoided the demand by always pleading he was waiting for payments from his creditors before paying off the bills. By 1939 there was 12 billion Reischmarks of the manufacturers and 19 billion of government bonds. Unfortunately, the national debt in 1939 was 39 billion marks, which Hitler blamed on the Jews, causing Kristalnacht, the persecution of the Jews. Hitler replaced Schacht with Goering in 1936 and Schacht continued with some type of title in order to collect a stipend from the government and live comfortably from then through the war. Schacht survived the Nuremburg War Crimes Trials, possibly because of his acquaintance with Thomas McKittrick, the U.S. lawyer who ran the Bank of International Settlements from 1939 to 1946, and ran a retail business afterwards in Dusseldorf until his death in 1970 (Trading with the Enemy by Charles Higham, 1983).

Another illustration of German adaptability took place in 2003 when France and Germany exceeded their budget deficits (they were over 3%GDP) and there was a decline in exports. Many members of the Common Union didn't want the headquarters placed in Germany, but fifteen members, including U.K. Gordon Brown's government, voted to let the countries off and against prevention due to the excess. The headquarters of the European Central Bank was placed in Frankfurt and Angela Merkel and the German government approved a 50 billion euro plan to rescue the German economy from the export decline, pleading that a decline would cause 200,000 job losses and hurt the economy for too long a time.

In 2013, inflation in Germany runs 1.8%, unemployment 5.3% out of an estimated work force of 44 million from a population in sixteen states of 82 million people. In 2012, Germany took in estimated revenues of $1.51 trillion and had expenses of $1.50 trillion. Germany is the third largest exporter in the world and devotes one third of its national output to export. It exports autos, metals, machinery and tools, chemicals, and Adidas shoes. Two-thirds of its energy is imported, like oil and natural gas, as well as machinery, vehicles, chemicals, foodstuffs, textiles, and metals.

Thirty-seven of the Fortune Global 500 companies are located in Germany. To name some: Volkswagen, Allianz, Daimler, EON, Siemens, Deutsche Telecom, BASF, BMW, Robert Bosch, ThyssenKrupp, MAN, Bayer, Merck, Adidas, Puma, Deutsche Bank, Henkel, Hugo Boss, Mercedes Benz, Audi, Porsche, Lufthansa, Nivea. Germany is also the leading producer of wind turbines and solar power technology in the world (Ask.com).

In 2006, the average gross salary in Germany was 4,217 euros ($5,692) but the net salary was 2,040 euros ($2,754) per month. Why the discrepancy? Because retirement in Germany is age 67 and taxes in France and Germany take out almost 50% from workers' wages plus the Value Added Tax on anything they buy. However, retirement in Europe furnishes almost as much as what a worker was earning in his take home pay. In Germany, a retiree with pension and social security gets 42%; in France 49%; in the U.K. 32%; in Italy, men 65% women 51%; in the U.S., where government depends more on an individual's private pension and savings, 39% (Complaining About Taxes by Tyler Duesden, May 23, 2011). American politicians like to knock European countries as being Socialistic but the countries don't give anything away. The financial markets, on the other hand, like to think of themselves as entrepreneurs but they gladly accept and plead for government bailouts.

What country do you think got hit hardest by the global economic crisis? It's the country that gave away foreign aid to other countries even though its industrial production was down and its stock market in decline – Russia !

If it wasn't for cheap credit from western banks and high oil prices by its Gasprom, its flat income tax of 13% and reduced profits tax, and new land and legal codes, all the vodka in Russia couldn't make its satellite countries stop wanting to leave Mother Russia for self-rule and independent economies. Its millionaires have found that by investing in other countries, their money is worth more than by bringing it back to Russia. The economy is so gangster-ridden that the long queue lines daily for basic commodities will continue to be the bane of Russia.

There was a very informative article in the Wall Street Journal of April 24, 2013 By ISDA explaining the economic situation in Asia. Our previous consideration of China brought out about how individual investors were fleeced out of much of their savings by the sellers of derivatives. This article by the ISDA reveals about the banking industry in Asia.

We saw how the Bank of China, regardless of the government's doing, helped Chinese businesses by doing foreign currency transactions with them by keeping the yuan within China and the renminbi outside. As U.S. and European banks have been coming in to set up third country branches and work in foreign markets, the rules of the game come into question and the debate concerns whether the local or international regulations are used in Pan Asian markets (China, India, Taiwan, Korea, Southeast Asia, Australia). Internationally, we have the EMIR (European Market Infrastructure Regulation) and Dodd-Frank (U.S.) as guidelines (Basel III comes under EMIR). The concern behind all this is compliance and the costs for doing it.

As of 2013, market competition is still on-going but as entrenchments solidify, the market gaps will be eliminated, or so is the hope. Cross-currency swaps are heavily traded but interest rate swaps are thinly traded in Pan Asia. The Chinese and Indian markets are illiquid and appear to be best handled by bonds for infrastructure growth needs, rather than by bank borrowings. China likes options, spot markets, and domestic swaps and derivatives. India likes domestic swaps and derivatives but Singapore prefers a synthetic bond market. Korea likes to use government bonds as collateral in any dealings but the worry is will there be a favorable outcome, considering its problems with North Korea and industrial parks there.

The ISDA "looks for Asia to continue to regulate derivatives tightly but take a practical approach towards products viewed as bringing economic benefits."

As was stated about the Chinese being industrious and overcoming diversity by it, is the will to work it out part of the Asian psyche? Again, time will tell.

An article in IberaAmerica Empresarial in September 18, 2013 stated that Brazil and Argentina are the leading countries in South America. Brazil has the largest economy in Latin America and the ninth largest export market in the world due to its mining, manufacturing, and software development. Paraguay and Uruguay are considered as opportunities for the future. Argentina outstrips Florida for cattle production on its pampas. The middle class is growing in all of South America and the population is relatively young. Peru and Chile, along with the others, look more to the United Kingdom and the British pound to have a favorable exchange rate for their pesos rather than the dollar.

There seems to be a fear of the interconnectedness of the banks in South America and Mexico as evidenced by their high interest rates and these countries considering themselves as developing countries supporting their own infrastructures but attracted to the credit card market because of heavy tourism to their countries.

Central America looks like a string on a map, connecting South America to Mexico. Unlike tying things together, Central American countries have a mess of different currencies and floating exchange rates that don't give them any advantage for gain with their export and import markets.

Mexico, on the other hand, has a stable currency and one of the highest per capita incomes in Latin America. Unfortunately, the top 20% on the income scale have 55% of the income in the country. Oil exports account for 11% of the total export earnings, and one-fifth of the workforce in the country is employed in agriculture which is only 4% of the GDP and mining is less than 2% of GDP (2003). The oil crisis back in 1970 which saw the U.S. with a 55 mph speed limit on its freeways caused a Mexican default on its debt but since then there has been no debt. In 1982, 1,000 state enterprises cut down to 200, allowing more private companies to operate and improve the economy. Every six years a new President is elected. Hopefully, one of these times somebody is going to come up with the right solution to improving the economy by increasing employment and wages by keeping employers in the country.

Can you blame investors for wanting to keep their money invested? What better way to try and avoid taxes, plus it increases profits by making more money. Paying taxes does loosen the money that was made by giving it to the government which can use it to develop a better economy but the opportunity is there to make up for what is paid out by making some more money, instead of trying to hide it in offshore accounts which can be hard to keep track of. Worse, though, when investing in derivatives and swaps and taking risks that mother nature won't destroy what man has built or trying to grow, and human nature, involving other personalities and cultures, won't cheat or steal, and hoping mathematical formulas will overcome adversity, nature, personalities, and cultures to deliver profits according to the times chosen. To transpose Warren Buffett's wisdom: you like shooting yourself in the foot because then you have a reason for sitting down.

Too many politicians know so little about finance that they believe derivatives insure against losses. How many even realize that offshore accounts are not illegal, only hiding money is. It's a distinction that the Swiss don't view as being distinct or anything illegal.

Sixty years ago it was expected that stockbrokers would be from a wealthy family so they could use their social contacts to acquire customers for the stock market. In the 1970s, the President of the U.S. who would later go on to resign his position because of election irregularities, was friends with unsavory characters like Bebe Reboso, a reputed mobster, and Robert Vesco, a swindler in shady deals who escaped to Costa Rica and Cuba to avoid prosecution for rounding up funds to invest in himself. In the 1980s, we mentioned earlier about how the government helped put the Savings and Loans out of business, and in the 1990s, how the junk bonds gave a lead in to the derivatives and swaps. Theoretically, derivatives allow for absolute growth where both parties gain relative to their previous position under normal circumstances, but as what happened in the 2007-2009 financial crisis, when defective products were sold without revealing the risk to investors, then a loophole has been created that causes a chain reaction of failures.

Government allows for deduction of losses on taxes but derivative losses have cut values in the economy that take years to restore. Value cuts back production as people perceive less need of goods even though demand is there. Ageing doesn't rush demand nor does danger even after catastrophe occurs unless people realize the value of what should be replaced or is needed. That is why big, bad brokers of Wall Street are selling derivatives like options to those little old widows of past brokers and corporate captains and generals, as well as anyone wealthy, with the soothing saying that you have a right to buy but you are not under any obligation to do so unless you choose to. These are new and different times, like, who do you think is going to be President in 2016? Or, when is the stock market going to hit 20,000? Or, when is Greece going to default? Or, when is the interest rate on savings going to be 5%? Are these any different than buying a lottery ticket? You see the difficulty of trying to get the government to outlaw derivatives and swaps or regulate them. You're not obliged to play but you have a right to do so if you want to. But you have to pay taxes on whatever you win.

When Alexander Hamilton was a young man dealing with trades in the shops in the Caribbean, he learned that there are many ways to cheat but once the reputation is gained, no long is there trust. When working with James Madison on the Federalist papers, Hamilton wrote: "Wherever a greater power is given, all attendant powers are given." This power is stated in the U.S. Constitution, Article 4 Section 8. The House of Representatives controls the budget and the debt. What we, the government, owe ourselves is within the power of the House to forgive and forget. What we owe the nations who have lent to us is due to them and we must pay them off. As Paul Krugman, the economist, states: "Austerity is self-defeating." We have certainly seen the truth of that in the economies of the European countries that have tried it. With the number one economy in the world, certainly we should be able to come up with a plan to pay off our debt without using austerity and still caring for our own by being faithful to the truths we hold dear, God and Country. Time will tell.

Who's Got the Money?

A Citizen's View of the Great Fraud

By

Phillip   Manson

www.ingramcontent.com/pod-product-compliance
Lightning Source LLC
Chambersburg PA
CBHW071004290526
45795CB00005B/1774